FAST TRACK YOUR BUSINESS

-18 Steps On Ideas, Marketing, Self And Employee Management-

Also by 'Muyiwa Osifuye

THE SMALL BUSINESS STARTER'S GUIDE
- Sharing 30 Years' Experience on How to Build for Success -

FAST TRACK YOUR BUSINESS

-18 Steps On Ideas, Marketing, Self And Employee Management-

'MUYIWA OSIFUYE

Copyright © 2016 by 'Muyiwa Osifuye

All rights reserved.

No portion of this book may be reproduced – mechanically, electronically, or by any other means, including photocopying – without written permission of the publisher.

ISBN-13: 978-1537247120
ISBN-10: 1537247123

Contact:
mosifuye@yahoo.com
contact@muyiwaosifuye.com

Stom and Ruby Services, Lagos, Nigeria
(Management Consulting / Business Advisory)
www.muyiwaosifuye.com

To

my eternal Muse,
as always – perpetual gratitude,

-

O, S & T
- my trio,

&

the memory of
"Mama Thomas"
- my doting Grandma, the first business-woman I ever knew

Contents

INTRODUCTION

PART ONE

CHAPTER 1
Where Great Business Ideas Come From ... 1
Three Major Fears ▫ Great Ideas Are Inside Of You ▫ Hidden Nuggets Of Gold ▫ Ideas From Outside ▫ Creativity and Innovation ▫ Innovative Ideas That Sell ▫ Specialization Dilemma ▫ The Rich And The Mass Markets

CHAPTER 2
Barriers To Ideas ... 20
Being Commonplace ▫ Regulatory & Cultural Limitations ▫ What If...? ▫ Managing An Innovative Team

CHAPTER 3
Selection & Validation ... 30
Steps To Your Best Idea ▫ Validating For Profitability

CHAPTER 4
The Need For Patience ... 38
The Twists And Turns

CHAPTER 5
Opportunities In K.I.S.S ... 42

CHAPTER 6
Ideas Worth Taming ... 47

PART TWO

CHAPTER 7
Define Your Market ... 55
Marketing Versus Selling ▫ Who Your Customers Are ▫ The Demographics

CHAPTER 8
Testing The Market ... 62
Pricing Can Be Romantic

CHAPTER 9
Don't Wink In The Dark ... 68
Getting The First Clients ▫ Direct Marketing ▫ A Smart Way To Get Customers ▫ Why Promotion? ▫ Public Relations ▫ Experiential Marketing ▫ The Art Of Selling ▫ Branding Beyond The Logo

CHAPTER 10
Surviving The Competition ... 81

CHAPTER 11
Perception And Location ... 87

PART THREE

CHAPTER 12
Managing The Most Delicate Asset ... 97
Managing Employee Relations ▫ Managing Employees: As Art & Science ▫ Your Team Can Kill Your Enterprise!

CHAPTER 13
Hiring And Firing ... 103
Recruitment Can Be Tricky ▫ Firing & Resignation

CHAPTER 14
The Manuals Of Operations... 114
The Best Management Style ▫ Employees Matters ▫ Team Commitment ▫ Big Companies & Team Management

CHAPTER 15
Managing Yourself – The Boss... 126
Your Business Will Change You ▫ The Fear Of Decision Making ▫ Watch Your Emotion ▫ Your Daily Grind

CHAPTER 16
Time In... 137
Managing Customer Interface ▫ Juggling The Working Capital ▫ Get Up From The Chair ▫ Getting Your Work Done ▫ The Modern Day Time-Stealers

CHAPTER 17
Time Out... 145
The Little Exercise ▫ Napping For Productivity ▫ Feeling The Blues

CHAPTER 18
Dealing With Problems... 149
Steps To Problem Solving ▫ Recognizing The Red Flag

Free Resources & Other Books ... 154

About The Author ... 155

Introduction

A successful entrepreneur is that person with a disciplined mind that is imbued with an insatiable craving for new knowledge, to promote and sustain profitable ventures into the future.

The aforementioned you may consider as a definition but let me quickly say here that these words just came to me. They came to me after days of ruminating over …who really is an entrepreneur - in my own words.

Since my MBA training in 1991 and as a practitioner in small business - over 30 years and still counting - I have come to a conclusion that there are 4 issues that are so fundamental for success.

This book has rather put them in 3 parts for clarity and to expose your mind to these basics. From here you can develop your own thoughts for accurate actions and decisions.

In no particular order, these issues are:

Ideas and Innovation,
Marketing and Sales,
Human Resources or Employees Management and
Self-Management for the Business Owner or Manager

The book is devoid of impractical business theories but offers my practical experience in the field. Other relevant insights into the world of business are also included.

As usual, the content might be deceptively lean but you will have been given a strong foothold and tips that would minimize major missteps. Enjoy…

PART ONE

Chapter 1

Where Great Business Ideas Come From

We are told that ideas rule the world! This is very true. However, you will be shown how to arrive at great ideas for your business.
In coming up with concrete ideas, many business owners seek such lists bandied around for their new venture.
Here are some questions many aspiring or existing business owners would ask, in the guise of discovering an exclusive idea…

I will list a few as follows:
"what business can I do?",
"how to get ideas for business?",
"the way to earn money…",
"what business should I start, with low startup capital?",
"how to make ideas real and profitable?",
"how to start a business with no money?",
"how to protect business ideas?",
"how to know if the idea is viable?",
"what is the best business idea in time of recession?"
and many more.
I can go on and on.

The deep seated meaning in these questions is that these individuals don't actually know how workable business ideas are arrived at.
They are looking for the simplest answers but ignore those that will be unique to them. They are thinking of a money making idea, that no other person is privy of. They want to beat other aspiring business owners or existing entrepreneurs to that lofty business idea.

Unfortunately it does not work that way. Such templates bandied around are too general and many have a copy or at least they are aware of such.

There are two major sources of ideas. They may come through our own circumstances and outside of us – that is, the external environment. But a truly worthy set of ideas for business cannot really be found in those so-called lists bandied around.
As you will see, they cannot take you far. They are just simple seeds shared by everybody. You need to discover your own but unique ideas that can bring you relative success.

Three Major Fears
Let me quickly address three major fears about why you may hesitate to bring an idea to the market place.

The first is thinking that your ideas would be stolen. That could be true. But you know what? In my own reckoning, there has never been a finished product or a completed idea. Your idea being stolen depends on its type and your industry.
I am not saying you should not keep secret, some creative ideas. However be consoled by the fact that it is the implementation or the execution that is the real beef. That is where the real work is.

Bringing ideas to the market place and sustaining them, is what matters. It is not every copycat that can do that very well, ultimately.
But I will advise – where feasible – that you use the laws of your country, to protect your creative work and ideas.

Be mindful that this effort might be expensive and it is not absolutely fool proof. And it also takes time to get the documentation done. It is your constant development of the idea, through innovative efforts that will put you ahead of the copycats. Your passion and continuous innovation are what would push you ahead.

The second reason why some people choose to sit on the fence is that, you wonder about your coming late into the market. You see so many competitors and you become discouraged.
But the question you should ask yourself is; are you sure there isn't any room for improvement, if you look very well?
In the same vein, don't be excited to rush in if there are very few players too. It could be there is something discouraging about that idea and the business. Therefore, you have to find out why. Because you will need to watch a situation where there are few competitors. Study that industry very well before coming to your conclusion.

The last reason of your hesitancy could be the fear that the idea might fail. Also that cannot be ruled out. That is a reality. In that case, you may be considering waiting until you come up with a perfect product to come out from your stable. The best advice is to come out with the minimum acceptable product. You can improve on that later.

But do believe that, no wise entrepreneur can ever be too sure of the success of any business idea, until you slog it out in the real world.
This is irrespective of all smart efforts and resources that must have been deployed. This is one of the known realities in entrepreneurship, which courageous business men and women are aware of.
All our efforts are simply adventures in risk taking. So take consolation in that.
You are not alone in your apprehension. Things may go wrong. But remember the cliché, "No pain, No gain".
Also you don't need to romanticize the popular saying that, we all learn and improve after a failed experience. That may be true, but let your

decision be well thought out and provide a room for plan B, should all else fails.
In other words, don't put all your eggs in one basket.

Great Ideas Are Inside Of You

Sometime in early 2015, I stumbled upon an article where the founder of *Vista Jet* was interviewed.
Thomas Flohr - the founder - narrated how he had identified a special need for more detailed attention by people who fly chartered private jets. As a client, he had had a disappointing personal experience. He felt he didn't get an optimum service.
Therefore, he researched further to discover that other patrons like him demanded that extra attention for details, he craved for. Despite being a harsh, risky and highly competitive industry, he plunged into the business to offer more flexibility to that small segment. So far, the business has been reported to be doing well.
Be rest assured that most of the so-called new ideas are not really original, but a hybrid of older or contemporary ideas. Most new ideas come about as a result of the synthesis, of all that have existed. These could be revealed from your subconscious. Some ideas might come to you as a hunch. Some people call it gut feeling or an instinct.

Recall the story about how the elusive chemical formula of *Benzene* was revealed to its discoverer (the scientist, *Friedrich August Kekulé*) in a dream. A school of thought is of the opinion that our subconscious mind would eventually push out what we ruminate over, after a period of time.
This statement may not be acceptable by everybody. But some people can swear on it as the truth.
I think the mind needs to be trained over time on this. After which you can consider what comes out, from within.

Fast Track Your Business

As for those who have such revelations, they must still test the ideas in the real world. And seriously speaking, there are a few people blessed with ideas that emanate through dreams. Think about that. Possibly you are gifted in that wise. Maybe.

An idea might be waiting to be extracted when we explore our own personal pains or needs for improved experience in our daily life. These may throw up business opportunities, especially those ideas that challenge the status quo. This could serve as a spark for an idea development, targeted at a segment of the society. In the same breadth that reminds me of a computer programmer who developed a computer *Application* for the restaurant business, after having worked as a waiter to understudy that industry.

Let it be known that innovative ideas may come to you, anywhere and at any time, when you least expect.

It may not necessarily be when you choose to hunk over a table, in your office. When they come save them as "sms" messages on your smart-phone, email these thoughts to yourself or voice record it on your phone. You may also choose to write these sparks of inspirations in your physical note pad if that's convenient. These sparks of ideas tend to disappear quickly as they come to you. If they are not written down quickly, you may not recollect them again.

Since ideas simply don't announce themselves, you may be wondering about how to come up with useful ideas. There are several ways to do this.

Let us look at it, this way.

Ask yourself about those things you personally want to experience but can't find around you. It could be you are going through some pains or you desire improvement in an aspect of your life.

No matter how mundane such thoughts might be to you; write them down for further examination as to their practicability

An entrepreneur is both a scientist and an artist whose imagination must soar all the time. You want to bring new things to the world – new vision about our world that will create improved values.
When you do this self-reflection and examination, ideas might crop up when you least expect – that quiet voice. It is most probable there is an ever increasing large market out there, with same wishes as yours.

Explore and test that idea to know if there is a deep market for it and its possible profitability. You will only take a plunge with your idea having done with validation.

However, do note that, only very few ideas would fly without adequate testing. Some products or services have come to be successful, taking this route by whim. Many small businesses take this risky path for lack of basic research knowhow. Others are simply impatient. Some lack adequate funds, manpower or technique of doing some survey. But I will advise you to do some test where practicable. This is always a better process to take to minimize risk.

Validation is a requirement to fine tune your novel idea. At this earliest stage, your thoughts are still raw. Kick away your romantic inner conviction of market acceptability.
Restrain your emotional jubilation of a *"eureka"*. *Don't run out from the bath*, thinking you have discovered a solution to mankind's problems. You don't deploy any resource at this early stage.

Hidden Nuggets Of Gold

That under-appreciated skill or knowledge you are blessed with but which appears insignificant to you, may be the solution to some real problems experienced by many people out there.

Many of us look down on these skills we have mastered over the years. We do so because they have become too familiar and are routine to us. That is where we miss it! These are activities other people see as a big problem or as inconvenient tasks for them to accomplish. Therefore, we naturally do not give a deep thought to them.

Another reason is that, while some of us are aware, we are simply shy or ignorant of how to market this endowment.

A quick advice: get or pay someone to market your skill for you.

So, search yourself by writing them down, what you think is "mundane" about your activities. They may be tangible or intangible. For example, you might have built alliances or networks over the years. This could be within your state, country or outside of it.

This network could be utilized as an economic opportunity of a comparative advantage. Leverage on it. You could use such relationships and connections to solve distribution challenges most business owners have.

Or bring two people together for a common cause. And get paid from both sides. Being well connected is an asset, which can throw up possibilities of good ideas too.

I will give you another scenario about individuals blessed with skills yet hidden. Many professionals have built processes and systems that have worked effectively in various industries.

Possibly you are one in your field. A well-oiled process or mastery of a system that renders faster and quality products is indeed, a welcome intangible asset – intellectual power.

This is a service that many setups could be interested in if it meets up with their expectations.

Another opportunity that beckons is a need to do a self-appraisal in terms of past experience of our failures and successes in life and business. You would have learnt from either of the two opposite experiences.

Anyone of them will put you in a good stead to help others from making same mistakes. It could be an affair of life.

Similarly you could easily help others to identify and grab opportunities in the offing, since you have the experience to smell such beforehand.

Personally speaking, I have gone through these diverse experiences – over 30 years in the entrepreneurship world and challenges in my personal life. This has therefore put me in a good position, to guide entrepreneurs in their business philosophy and personal life.

Despite the semblance of existing solutions in the market place, personal experiences are always more practical and realistic.

Think about all these things!

Ideas From Outside

On particular popular book-selling website, I read about a guy who makes cool money on a theme idea for children stories. He had earlier tested this idea on his nine year-old son, who very much enjoyed them. Thereafter, he assumed other kids within that age bracket would like the theme. Luckily his hunch proved him right.

Since then, he has been self-authoring a series on this funny theme while smiling to the bank. This idea development came as a result of a keen observation of his external environment. Outside of ourselves, our environment could reveal much for innovation. This we could develop

further into business opportunities.
From common and repeatable societal complaints and expectations, business opportunities are abound. Painstaking studying of various segments of the society reveal much. You should study deeply the fad, lifestyle, trends and beliefs at whichever location you want to test our ideas. It could be within your neighborhood, state, across the country local, or global.

We have to look out for the good and bad experiences of consumers that are in need of solutions and further tweaking for improvement.
For instance, today there are people who now accept that painting and other art works can be bought online. A few years back, it was never a popular channel by most of these collectors.

Saatchionline, Fine Art America - that have some of my personal works for sale - and other art galleries are slugging it out on the Internet.
Tastes of collectors and fallouts of global economics have changed the tradition in many areas of our life today. Physical art spaces are becoming more difficult to manage profitably; therefore the Internet has become an additional platform to be considered.

Imagine PayPal™, in spite of the inherent risks to the organization, still ensures smooth online transactions across the world.
Sadly though, as I write, the company is still apprehensive of my country, Nigeria, by leaving her out of the full experience. PayPal's innovative solution to global financial transactions goes on despite the traditional mediums of monetary exchange which they met in the industry.

You never can tell about possibilities out there, if one looks hard enough. In essence, if one observes closely, the societal nuances reveal much

about money making possibilities. Events in the society throw up ideas in disguised manners.
They may not be earth shaking in their outlook but could be very rewarding with time.

Government, political and socio-economic challenges do throw up opportunities as new ideas for start-ups. Sadly, some of these will include terrorism and extreme beliefs, especially religion. New doctrines and ideologies are not excluded.
These are our unfortunate realities of today. But as infamous as they are, it is an invitation to finding ways to solving these problems in all their ramifications.
As unwelcome as some of these global trends have become our reality, there are smart entrepreneurs who analyze this reality, to develop new product ideas.
New technologies also throw up opportunities for idea development. If we recall, when the *iPad* came out, somebody was observant enough, to produce simple covers for them. A *Patrick Buckley* took calculated actions to test his *dodo* cases and the venture has made good income as reported. For those looking for home-based businesses, there are opportunities for working from home, if you take the time to reflect on this book very well.

I will repeat: business ideas do not have to be earth shaking.
Simple beginnings are much easier to get started. Thereafter you may choose to get bigger; at least you will have some bucks in your coffer before trying bigger things.
You can always start on something so basic, as long as it solves a significant problem of the society.

On the other side of the coin, one needs to be wary of the disruptive tendency of technology, which could make an existing but successful idea, to become suddenly obsolete.
As nothing is permanent, the concurrent reality brings new opportunities. As a matter of fact, we should be able to make accurate projection of the consumer's future needs – before he or she realizes that need.

The environment often gives us business opportunity leads, if we reflect much beyond the obvious.
Remember the McDonald hamburger franchise is a classic example. The popular story was that the founder saw beyond the hamburger. He saw the possibility of replication, like an assembly line.
A process that could churn out in a predictable manner, a food product of same taste, size and weight that could be replicated in any outlet.

I remember in 1994, I used to have these nagging thoughts about young mothers and the need for medical insurance scheme in Nigeria. It was non-existent then.
I realized that young and educated working mothers would eventually need the services of formal crèche setups. This was because the traditional helping hands – that hitherto were not educated coming from the villages in the hinterland – had been dwindling in numbers. And still is, because of improved education and awareness.

Then I also thought of security video-cameras that would enable mothers at work to remotely monitor their kids at the crèche. Widespread telephony and Internet penetration only became prominent after 2001.
I think my wild but seemingly impossible thoughts - as they were - have become a reality in a few crèches today.
The second idea, as a practicing optometrist - with my own clinic, I saw a need for a health insurance scheme. In the same 1994, I wrote, I think,

the *International Health Insurance* in London. They replied me to say they were not ready for Nigeria which did not even have a scheme in place until now.

Invariably I lost interest in that idea as it developed. I could have been one of the players in that industry. Today for those involved in that line of business, it appears they have been doing well in Nigeria. Now we have the scheme in place.

What I am getting at is that, ideas generally in any industry or in any aspect of our lives can be scanned with all our senses. Namely by what we see, hear, touch, taste and how we feel as entrepreneurs.

A *Mr. Elon Musk* rubbing shoulders with *NASA* through his *Space X* company, as we are made to believe.

Let's illustrate with a little exercise here…

Imagine how some people would react to a fabric, leather or other types of texture finishing, which has never been used for a particular piece of furniture.

That could be a revolutionary idea, as subtle as it is. A mere change from the popular color known for a traditional piece of furniture could arouse curiosity. An idea that could eventually lead to increase in sales. You never can tell what will sail through, in the market place until you test it.

If you look within your neighborhood, you can see some businesses that have lost out, to a more polished service due to superior ideas, within that same industry. And since the loyalty of an average customer is shaky, they will move on to a more pristine shore.

You will discover new ideas by mere but conscious listening to people and groups of people. You must discover the root cause of people's behavior, which may be different from what they are actually projecting.

I am not too sure if the late *Steve Jobs* actually uttered that…*consumers generally didn't know what they wanted!* You may not entirely agree with this declaration if true. On the other hand, you should be asking yourself, "What do they REALLY need beyond what they are voicing out?"

Feel the environment beyond the cacophony of "noise". Search for the deep meaning. That's your job as an entrepreneur, to break things down to the elements. But verify and validate before you can conclude on your inference. This may reveal good business opportunities, if you analyze them very well.

For instance, getting somebody to cut your lawns and do your laundry means your time is more valuable to do such things. Not because you are incapable. If you are an aged fellow, health issues might be the reason and not necessarily because of affordability.

Studying the root cause of societal behavior can reveal actual needs. A casual observation of that person next to you may reveal a need for a service or product. Her disposition may be representative of a large market segment, waiting to be served.

Examples are many of successful ideas that came from the least expected places and circumstances.

And that's why I would call successful *entrepreneurs as sleuths of opportunism.*

Revelations of problems yearning to be solved could emanate from your spouse, kids, partners, family and friends or from total strangers. Search for repeated complaints by human beings, anywhere they aggregate, online and offline. Of course, they don't have to be big complaints.

Complimentary ideas may be served together to give a very powerful combo product – a hybrid of sorts. Imagine the dad-author I mentioned earlier; he could do what is called a brand extension.

He could get hold of a visual artist to make cartoons of the characters in those children books. This he can produce in different formats even as toys.

He may even get a producer to make jigsaw puzzles out of this seed idea. He may set up a website to provide free but interesting content to attract huge traffic from kids. This traffic can be monetized or content made free or as he deems fit. He can sell complimentary products branded in the characters of his stories and sell them through the website.

The author can outsource these ideas while he concentrates on churning out more stories.

The possibilities of a spinoff are there to be considered, provided you can manage the offshoots through assistants. Business idea development is as vast as an entrepreneur can stretch his mind.

You don't have to do everything yourself. Successful entrepreneurs know it is important to collaborate with others for effectiveness. Be a good conductor of an orchestra of your team who would bring your ideas to reality.

Creativity And Innovation

There is a need to make a quick clarification. As defined, creativity that is welcomed by your market niche can be regarded as an innovation.

In the market place, you can't be creative for the sake of it. If you do so, that exercise is simply for your own personal enjoyment, if the market is not receptive to it.

Probably the product features, the timing, the audience or location is simply not right, at the period in question. However, when the market – always self-centered – appreciates your novel efforts and is willing to pay for it, then it can be said you have come up with an innovative idea.

Only your targeted market will applaud you and vote for your product with their money and with words of referrals to others.
It means you have eliminated their pains or your idea has brought improvement to their existence. However, all these are still subject to other external factors. Look for clues in taste for trends, lifestyle, and prevailing culture and maybe future culture – what will they most likely be willing to pay?

A well accepted innovative idea may not be all that elaborate but could be a simple twist of a product and the market could love it very much. It doesn't have to be an earth shaking exercise in other words.
An intangible idea may be as simple as; a rehearsed set of phrases that are uttered by your staff when they receive your clients.
It may be the arrangement of the restaurant chairs to achieve a purpose. You can experiment on your own.
The simple objective is to increase customer's satisfaction and this could shoot up dwindling sales when measured after the deployment of the idea.
Innovation can also be applied to other areas such as process development and building of business systems.

For instance, it may involve a few twists of the traditional way of doing things. It could be a new set of guidelines of hiring staff, reaching out to prospects or finding new ways of reducing costs in the business.

The expanse of innovation is as wide as the imagination of a visionary – the entrepreneur. That is, if the entrepreneur allows his or her imagination to be elastic. Going by the popular saying; if you know the rules, you may break them, ethically. That gives you further creative freedom. That is one of the secrets of past pioneers in many areas of human endeavors.

This courageous mindset of innovators and creative people has brought about breakthroughs. If you fail, you are far better off than those sitting on the fence.

The wisdom there is to make your calculated foray. But the challenge is to fine-tune your raw thoughts. They must be subjected to the needs of the market, as I would always advice.

That is the test of reality.

I know that while trying to cope with competition - by fine-tuning a better customer experience - all sorts of new twists of ideas will be going on in your mind. You need to calm down and manage the situation objectively.

Innovative Ideas That Sell

Let me share a personal experience, which occurred sometime in early 2015. I had some items in my personal inventory for a while. The product till now has a very good profit margin. For some reasons I was not positioned to sell directly to potential customers.

The items were just lying down there, staring at me. I have such items like that. Outside my core business, I thought I could make some regular cash by the side from this product and that got me thinking.

A new e-commerce platform, a website, which has been dominated by other types of products, just came on board in my country. I was wondering how my products would get patronized in the midst of competition.

I did not want to compete on price (reduction) with similar items. I knew I had some comparative advantages over the other online merchants selling the same items.

Due to my expertise, I could give more derailed and relevant descriptions of each item. This was not done very well by other merchants.

So I had an edge. I went further to develop a combo package without increasing the average price. No other merchant was offering a bundle of items.
Can you guess the result of this experiment? My inventory was sold within the first week I tested this idea. When the sales stabilized after a month, I tinkered with the prices by increasing them a little, yet the sales did not drop. I maintained these prices without pushing them much higher than competition. This encouraged me to get more supplies.
This is an example of how intuition and acceptable creativity meets a need that sells.

Making a cocktail or hybrid of ideas could be another way out to have a unique package in your hands.
Great business ideas may be packaged as an admixture of products and services as your offering.
If you are into physical products, you could add a complementary but intangible service to it and vice-versa. You will see aerobic trainers that sell gym products; same with hair and beauty salons that sell different products. It is a simple form of diversification from the main offering. Also make efforts to ensure your idea is unique to a large extent. You don't want your efforts to become a flash in the pan, but an enduring one.

Specialization Dilemma

Let's look at why we should be careful about over-specialization even though there is strength in this approach of giving out the best; there is. Imagine you have deployed all resources in a relatively expensive location, selling a single but simple item.
Picture that you have an ice cream place in a hot tropical country. What about when the wet season comes; you are likely to find that patronage

dwindles. In your strategic planning before you start such a venture, you ought to have considered you will also be making coffee or tea in anticipation of the rainy season. This will be supported by other complimentary products or services that could go with both types of drinks. The possibilities are endless – within your imagination – provided the market needs them.

The cliché, *"Jack of all trade, master of none"*, may not be applicable to you if you are blessed with multiple skills or interests. More so if your proficiency is above average in every case. Make use of all of them.

This approach might not work very well for everybody. No sweat about that. You can still succeed in what you know, very-well. Dwell on that single one but watch it…one stream of income is never safe. Add things in stages as you master every business ideas - maybe two or three years down the line. But in some industries, it is advisable to concentrate on one or just a few competences.

Many companies routinely outsource some of their processes because they are more effective that way.

For example, there are businesses that come up with an idea. Part of the production if not all, is outsourced and made to their specification. Their brand name is then slapped on the finished product. This is a very common business model. Car manufacturing industry easily comes to mind. And many others.

The Rich And The Mass Markets

Let's look at customers that belong to different economic strata. How do you position your business? If your business is targeted at those at the lower rungs of the economic ladder, it does not mean your business will be miserable. If that market segment runs into millions, even at marginal profit, you could still make your good money.

This becomes possible, if you have the capacity and capability to service this large number, which must be supported by good product formulation amongst others things.

On the other hand, should you wish to be involved in a high end or luxury market that will demand a different strategy.

You will be asking a few questions, such as:

What is the population of this market segment - will it be deep enough?
What is the purchase cycle; within a time frame?
That is, how frequent - on average - does a customer return to make another purchase?
And do you at the material time have all the resources to address the sentiments and the mannerism of such sophisticated customers?

If you nurse such a business in your portfolio, there is a way to go about this, when the idea strikes you.
You will need to first nurture the modest enterprise you have at hand into sustained profitability. Later on, you might take a portion of your reserved funds and invest in such an exotic business.
If your exclusive idea works, then you are lucky. Should it fail, you can still fall back on the goose that lays the golden eggs. Since you have not killed the little fish in your search for the giant whale, you will have something to fall back to.

Chapter 2

Barriers To Ideas

Have you considered if it is easy for just any competitor to enter into your line of business? There are ideas that have low entry barriers, which make competition very stiff. It will be a sad future if a competitor comes in and provides a much better service. This might make your business ultimately irrelevant if care is not taken.

Such a business idea may be dropped, unless your strategic objective is to quickly make some profit and thereafter exit as soon as possible.

Being Commonplace

If the idea is commonplace - and not really unique in its outlook, then you would be competing with others - so seriously. Nearly all of the players will sell at the lowest prices eventually. An all comers affair with low barrier of entry tends to be the easiest to copy.

Cutting prices - otherwise known as price war – is the most common tactic. Not a very profitable one for all players at the end of the day, I must say. You are all probably selling at the same level of quality. Your services are equally positioned the same way in the eyes of the consumer. If you continue in this manner, your business will not do well into the future.

And you should be asking; *"Are there ways of resolving this problem"?*
There are, of course.

As I had mentioned before, one of the options is to add a complimentary product or service to your initial offer. Scan around for an additional offer that is very exclusive to you – that gives your business a comparative advantage. It could also be a product that you have sourced, at a negotiated discount, through an alliance with another business partner. Sell the combo at a price less than the total, each item would have sold separately.

Another option is to continue with the original business idea until you discover another one, with a higher barrier of entry. And continue with both, if profitable collectively.
You may want to diversify into another line of business which gives you a better comparative advantage – that may have a higher barrier of entry.

Yet another extreme idea; you can relocate to another well-thought-out location where there is little or no competition. This could be a tough decision but it might be your saving grace.
Do a very good business and personal appraisal before making this move - literarily speaking. Be sure such a movement is profitable and will be worthwhile on the long run. Such an action supports the fact that ideas could be very intangible, that is, by this movement.

In my own case, some years back, I took a drastic step in starting a business with a different business model from what I had planned. There was a reason for it. From the blues a competitor beat me to the same location where I really wanted. I delayed because I was yet to raise the minimum starting capital.

This brings to mind, when you look around and you wonder why many people shy away from investing in a seemingly profitable type of business or industry. I am talking about a business opportunity which might look attractive to your own naïve eye, until you get closer.

There could be unforeseen barriers put in place, as a competitive strategy by the existing players. It could also mean those stuck there barely make enough profit. As the popular sayings goes... *they want out*, but they may not courageous enough to start another business or move elsewhere. While some of such businesses may be at the brink of declaring bankruptcy – which might not be the situation - they may still choose to stay on. They linger on with the hope of a positive shift in the business horizon.

The lesson here is to watch out for a business or industry you have not investigated properly. It makes smart sense to do a prior study of that industry very well no matter how attractive it might appear to you.

Anybody can brand *Tee* shirts for sale or cut the lawn but it takes a while to become a lawyer or a successful marketer or a salesman. That is the reason why good money is made in strictly highly skilled professions or businesses where the entry barrier is high.

There are noticeable examples as can be seen in advanced technology, manufacturing, delicate medical surgeries, inventors, even in soldiering. All these can't be compared to selling coffee at a sidewalk.

You must add something to that to stand out. Anyhow, if your brand of coffee is exotic to the palate of thousands around your market, you could stand out. But you would do better, if you could add more ideas so that your business would not be commoditized.

What do I mean by that?

Let that coffee business be about a properly *defined experience* from the perspective of your prospects, beyond just selling a product.

As reported this is how some coffee shops in Australia have survived *Starbucks*? This increased barrier has allowed the local operators to open shop despite this big sized company.

Regulatory & Cultural Limitations

Now that you have mooted an innovative idea, have you looked at the legal and cultural limitations? The idea must conform.

Your locale, state or country would influence the final product before your full launch.

A company may need to modify its creative ideas to meet the legal requirements of the state. You will see such examples in the medical, pharmaceutical and food industry.

New products, procedures or surgical techniques must get legal backing from local regulatory agencies and even professional bodies.

This equally applies to small-business owners and micro-entrepreneurs in their respective levels. There should not be any exceptions to these rules for consideration by any serious business owner.

No matter how attractive your innovation is, even if the populace is yearning for it, it must be permitted by these watchdogs.

Recall the recent *Ebola* outbreak in West Africa – late 2014 and early 2015. It became a dilemma, whether or not to use a drug - not yet fully approved - by the American Food and Drug regulatory authority, as we read in the papers.

While the outbreak ravaged on, there were infected people including American missionary health workers stationed in Liberia, who were at the point of death. The infected American missionaries were returned to the US for treatment. It was said those that recovered were given some shots of this drug but it was not released elsewhere, according to the global media. There could be a possibility that it had not passed through all the test-requirements.

This also brings to mind, the issue about cloning. It has been claimed in some quarters, that a human being can be replicated. Glad to say that most countries have openly refused the full exploration of this idea. Sentiments have been based on the moral and ethical implication of this sensitive undertaking.

However, a monitored regulation has been given to the practitioners of the stem cell research with its derived benefits. Whereas some countries won't even touch this particular discovery, despite its life-saving results. This is due to the influence of local culture, tradition and belief system.

The acceptance of a creative idea is also subject to the cultural behavior of that immediate society. The people have to be mentally ready to accept a new idea and how they generally interpret its usefulness in their lives. An idea rejected elsewhere, may be accepted in another clime. Businesses that want to operate in multi-locations must take note of these cultural restraints in their strategic planning.

What If…?

Some of us are given to good hunches, exclusive of any research efforts. Just by mere observation over a period of time, with adequate experience, we "know" inside of us if an idea would fly, in the market place.

But there are instances where a proper investigation or the suitability of an idea must still be carried out. It might be done on a low scale or as in the case of the conglomerates; they do theirs on a larger scale.

And for some reasons, when the business starts, an erstwhile successful idea may fail for many unforeseen.

Unexpected factors may truncate a good business idea – sometimes we can't seem to explain some reasons.

Imagine a scenario that goes thus. You have found yourself in an area or neighborhood that appears fertile for your outfit. Such a location has been fully researched by you in anticipation to start a business.

In addition if you think it is a good spot for an hotel, say; a bed and breakfast. Much has been invested so much in resources and emotional capital. Now you sit back expecting to start raking in streams of income, within two years or so.

And something suddenly happens!
The local council or government – not out of mischief – but for the general good of the citizenry has decided to construct a road, right through your hotel's premises. And you were simply just settling down!!
In some parts of the world, you may be given some monetary compensation, which may be a difficult thing to come-by in other places.

That could lead to an endless legal battle to get compensated. When the latter is eventually done, the money might not be adequate. This usually results in other losses that may not be monetary in nature.

In some countries you may not even get paid at all. You might even be in debt of legal fees and finding yourself entrenched in other forms of unwarranted pains and pending obligations.
This is why I advocate a mindset when one is going into business, to repeatedly abide by my mantra.
The, *what if...?*.

Essentially, this is not about being pessimistic but being realistic too. It has kept me away from heartaches and debilitating health issues. And we entrepreneurs must really do all we can to avoid ill health, which most are prone to.

Managing An Innovative Team

Idea development within a group of people such as a team or in bigger organizations can be a real challenge. It is also a sensitive issue to the survival of a business of whatever size.

To develop a good system for an effective idea development program, there is a need for proper management of both the internal and external factors.

However, continuous tinkering with existing products is very important for a company's long term survival. As the enterprise grows from infancy to adolescence and matured phases, you have more people to contend with in a group.

This exercise will usually throw up some friction; where there is a consensual need to agree to new ideas and product development.
If we take it closer to a family setting, you can't even rule out such a friction in a husband and wife working together on their business, when crucial decisions have to be made.

And how do we handle novel ideas that are suggested by a few individuals in such a big company?
Same question could be asked in small outfits too? Because a creative idea at first might appear untenable, such that the particular contributor might have some self-doubts.

This is how to manage innovative ideas within a group:
The individual that comes up with the idea needs to really investigate it objectively. This has to be done, devoid of any ego trip or sheer sentiments.
Be ready for an honest critique by others. The idea should be supported for "further investigation" by others but not out of mischief.

The idea should not be rushed to the trash bin. The creator cannot be disregarded or made fun of, no matter stupid the idea might be. This objective approach would help a sensible company in its entrepreneurial journey.

If collaborations are missing, many breakthroughs may not see the light of the day. Such companies could easily discourage the gifted from volunteering new ideas. A lot of companies have gone under because there is no system in place to encourage individual's creativity.
(I don't need to list the popular companies in this unfortunate group, but they are well known).

Asking a group in particular to come up with new ideas collectively, may be an exercise in futility in many setups. If you must, adequate care must be put in place to manage group social behavior.
Brainstorming by a group, done within the same space and allocated period will simply become a merry-go-round affair. An exercise in futility - of motion without movement. And nothing is achieved, if care is not taken during and after such sessions.

If you would, there is a need to set up a guideline or an agenda to remove possible self-inflicted obstacles – by the group – in order to arrive at timely recommendations.
Such guidelines agreeable by all must be designed to downplay each member's ego. There is a need to arrive at a collective and an agreeable idea. Some members who may not have much to contribute at a particular session should not be disregarded, because you can't force genuine inspiration.
Reasons for this could be due to diverse individual personalities, experiences and influence of strong posturing by other participants. Silent conflicts may be created which could slow things down.

Opinions of those regarded as dissenters, non-conformists or rabble-rousers should still be respected – within reasonable means.
Their submissions must be objectively studied and never a rush to get them discarded.
This is to avoid *Groupthink* – a social psychological phenomenon – that could be noticeable within a group of people.
It is a mindset associated with entrenched groups that share common beliefs. Members tend to think alike, at times, at the group's detriment.
A lone voice that suddenly has a spark of inspiration – contrary to the group's tradition – may be shouted down.
In retrospect that suppressed voice could be the savior against an impending problem or an opportunity that ought to be taken up.

When an idea has been agreed upon, resources must be deployed immediately for implementation. A time frame is applied to test the idea and inference must be made from results received.
If the outcome meets the parameters of the overall pass mark, the creator of the idea ought to be congratulated. It is also important that all the other participants must be applauded too.
Without contributions from other participants, there is no way the selected idea would have been appreciated.
Likewise, the chosen idea must be discussed across the organization, down to the factory floor. Complete collaboration and patience will be needed, to allow the idea work its full course of testing.

In many ways, the innovative exercise in an organization should be an all-inclusive affair. Everybody should be celebrated when it eventually brings a positive outcome.
Otherwise, if some members of the team are ignored, this sends a bad signal and prevents future cooperation.

The creator of the seed idea must be compensated. The management should extend a weighted means of appropriating compensation across board amongst the contributors. This stimulates others to be motivated. They will see themselves as co-contributors and not as mere bystanders. This approach reduces any form of rivalry but gives the needed chivalry for the team.

Personally speaking, I am not an advocate of group creative exercises, where people are put together inside a room, to come up with ideas, within a time frame.
That is what I am saying here.
I'd rather all individuals, were briefed to come up with their personal and isolated ideas, when there are issues the company wants to address.
These ideas will be annotated anonymously and investigated for usability by all stakeholders at scheduled meetings. The best idea is considered!

Chapter 3

Selection & Validation

What are the big issues here?
At the end of the day, it is about values in the eyes of your consumers. It is all about profitability and survival of the business and acceptance by the place or location your business is situated.

You don't select ideas for the sake of it. You might soon get burnt.
You must find out the nuances or the subtle needs of your prospects and how to serve them profitably.
You want to discover the big help needed, by your potential customers. This will be matched with the appropriate strengths and core skills found in your enterprise.
That would stimulate your passion which will also be needed to sustain the business through its rocky life cycle. (This is assuming you have discovered a willing market niche waiting to be served, and willing to pay). When this has been achieved, this brings about mutual benefits between the business and the consumer.

Steps To Your Best Idea

Since ideas can be superfluous and for them to work as desired, it is advisable you do a little test to affirm acceptability. Most of these ideas will not be useful but you will be better off than someone who does not stimulate his or her mind to pen than a few.
This will be carried out within your market niche or segment.

And if you have the resources, repeat the exercise using the same parameters in a similar market elsewhere.
Study the feedback. That experience may serve as an opportunity to modify and test again. If it works, then that will be good news for you. You can now plan towards further trial testing before the full launch.

Pick a pencil and start writing down spuriously what ideas come to your mind. There are times the sparks of inspiration may not be immediate; do respect that. As a matter of fact, it is very rare as one sits down and decides to conjure up really great business ideas, at the snap of the fingers. It doesn't work that way, always.
As you write, do not at this stage criticize the usability of those ideas. Wait till the next day or more and start appraising them, subject to relevant criteria. Fine-tune the reality of each one. Make a selection of the best five or less.

Systemically think them through in your mind in reference to your predetermined criteria and finally pick one to test.
This chosen one *may* be the one. I say…*may*.
Keep the other three or four ideas at bay for possible future reconsideration, in case the first does not fly very well over time.

Make sure your friends or loved ones are not the ones telling you, if it is a perfect idea or a wrong idea. Most times they tend to be wrong.
Let the objective answer come from the market place.
You may need to spend some money to test, at different physical locations, inclusive of the Internet - if this platform is applicable to your business.
Let me use this opportunity to reiterate that, despite the onslaught of internet based businesses, there are wide business opportunities in the physical, brick and mortar world.

Consider what I will coin as the *"brick and click"* business model. That is a physical business that also uses the Internet as one of its additional platforms for business success. A simple single webpage might just be what such a business might need, as an online resource and tool.

Do not be carried away with only the internet based businesses. Many needs of the human race are still more real than virtual. If you are a farmer, you have to do the physical work, right? The web presence will be used as additional publicity of your farm produce and your business.

Back to our topic…
Before you set out in your test marketing efforts, just like in any department of your business, you must consider quite a few things.

Do have a check list of what you want to achieve.
It is possible your hunch might be agreeable with the needs of the market. But be cautious before you deploy all resources blindly in execution.
Do not fall in love with your hunches until you validate.
Know the psychological makeup of your prospects.
Remember that money making ideas are not really about you, the producer.
The decision and power belong to the consumer. Of course there are occasions where you as the producer, may psychologically influence customer buying decisions. We see that happens.
But you must get things done right. This is very common with high profile goods and services targeted at the super rich. If you can feed their ego – that tends to work – but be aware that no consumer is stupid.
But for the mass market, they are damn stubborn psychologically. They would scrutinize your product for every cent, kobo and farthing.

Validating For Profitability

After the selection, the next step is to develop the ideas into concrete products and other offerings.

For commercial ventures, validation is an exercise you must carry out to confirm that the idea will sell profitably.

Determine the amount of resources and capital – both human and material – that you will need to do your testing.

Test for the depth of the market niche. The population of the expected consumers must be large enough to guarantee adequate supply and patronage into the future.

This segment of the population must also be big enough to accommodate other future competitors. Otherwise you may have to drop the idea or modify it. You must also confirm that the prospective customers have the financial capability and willingness to pay. These last two factors are sacrosanct.

So how do you go about validating an idea?

Start with the minimum viable product, MVP. *(A sensible concept conceived by a gentleman - but not by me, though).* It means you start with a product idea that gives minimum customer satisfaction.

Note that, it is not every idea that can be practicable, to be produced for validation. It might be studied through feedback from surveys, a questionnaire or a dialogue with prospects.

Now back to MVP. You can always tinker with this over time, with improved and additional benefits - as feedbacks are received from existing customers.

Before you deploy any significant resource, let a sample of your target consumer use or try out the idea.

You may have to practically leave your comfort zone to move into the trenches, outside to carry out this exercise successfully.
However if you are the shy type or for some reasons you can't go out, pay people and let them do it for you. But you must monitor the exercise.

Don't test your ideas amongst friends and family members. They will most likely be biased and won't be objective, ok? And again, they might not be representative of your target market.
Getting across to a carefully chosen group or individuals who fall into the definition of your target consumers, is a better route to take.
Additionally where practicable, include relevant retailers that serve your potential consumers. Get their feedback.

As an aside, listen very well to all feedbacks and understand what they are saying. This sounds simple but it is difficult for many people.
Personally, I am just overcoming this shortcoming myself; to really listen to understand and keep my mouth shut!
Advantages would include your discovering the real meanings behind what the prospects are saying.

Tabulate the field responses - whether online or offline.
The list of questions would include open-ended, direct and indirect types.
If it's possible anonymous feedback is more reliable.

Do not take the feedbacks personal, even if you are not happy with some of them. Better be sad now, than *fail* later into bankruptcy.
Feedbacks tend to bring up the need to slightly modify your initial idea. Respect this; and work on it.
Nothing to be ashamed about but it is a cause for thanksgiving. Now you know their needs much better than what you envisaged.

Don't be surprised if the majority of the feedback indicates a need for a toned down product, hence a reduced cost of production for you.
On the other hand, the field results could scream for additional features. This would entail additional cost of production you didn't bargain for – to really make an impact.
If you don't have the extra funds, then you will wait or find a creative solution within and outside the box.
Decide on what to do but be careful. It is not every time you throw available money at solving problems. The solution might just be, to being creative again, without spending additional resources or doing so for much less.

Abundant supply of resources may not necessarily guarantee the success of a business idea. I remember a side small business I targeted at kids. It came with a simple packaging.
We sampled schools, but they preferred a more robust package. However the schools did not want to pay for the slight increase in price? So we decided to face a different market segment – mostly individual parents – who were pleased with the basic packaging.

Another smart move in validation; depending on the idea, some entrepreneurs will advertise a non-existent product.
They publicize what they are yet to produce. The feedback gives them the true picture if they should go ahead to produce or not.
It is much easier to try this little trick, if its possible using the internet platform as well.
In the brick and mortar business, that is the physical location, a similar approach can also be used.

However do note that, despite the positive validation at full launch, the outcome might go either way. This is not the time to be squeamish.

You must identify the reasons. This includes your validation process and your feedback notes. Conclude on how the outcome can be modified. Decide if it will fly eventually, despite the rocky beginnings.

And painfully, there might be very cogent reasons why you need to abandon the idea and cut your losses. You may reconsider to re-launch this idea in the future or at a different location.
This goes with the assumption that, you or your team was not the main culprit – indirectly responsible – if the outcome is below expectation.

Now let us assume that after a successful launch, where all signs are encouraging; how do we proceed further?
There must be a culture of continuous strategic improvement of great customer experience of our offerings over time. I must admit this is tough in reality. But we have no choice but to strive. Otherwise our businesses would lose out eventually.

I like how *"Application"* developers market their products. They release the first – *beta* they call it – a basic version at a modest price. In some cases they are given as free. As the product goes through its life cycle – with all the feedbacks – these developers add more juice and sell at a premium price eventually.

Don't fall for too much perfection. Perfection may delay your coming out. Start with the minimum idea that is acceptable in the eyes of your prospects. Then improve with time. We have seen how *Facebook* overtook *MySpace*. Google has openly done better than Yahoo! as a search engine.
We have seen how these champions evolved over time in addition to servicing other secondary needs of its primary consumers.
At the initial stage of their entry, they handled rudimentary services.

Put it at the back of your mind, that a business is regarded as a "going-concern". Your starting ideas are your babies or seedlings that ought to grow through different stages into maturity.

Be mindful when all well thought-out plans fail. At times challenges may go beyond what the entrepreneur can cope with or comprehend. It happens. It can be terrifying and confusing for a hard working entrepreneur.
When your business is down, you become confused, more lonely and despaired. A few times you simply can't explain the reason for failure or that success.

Few years back, on a personal note, I ran two businesses which did well over the years. Suddenly they continued to fail. I did everything to improve the situation of things, no positive result.
In retrospection, I know I tried all I could to raise the nose of my entrepreneurial plane, it still crashed. Nevertheless, I learned quite a few things from the excruciating experience.

Today, the advantage is that I could recognize, much better, the signs of an impending red flag, before it appears in the horizon. Still, there would be near misses but you get better, based on prior experience.
The lesson: you can't know the future with all certainty.

And talking about success; when all the ideas seem to be coasting home as expected…be thankful.
On his unprecedented success, Paulo Coelho - the superstar author was asked - what was the secret to his selling mega-millions of his works?
He replied that he couldn't put a finger on a reason.
But he submitted that he wrote each work, with love and passion.

Chapter 4

The Need For Patience

We may rush to conclude on the outcome of an innovative idea, especially if the results are not quickly yielding fruit as expected. More so, if much has been expended - both in human and financial resources.

When we have agreed on a creative idea, there is a need to give it time to yield results. We give it time to see how the market accepts it. This gives the opportunity for a more robust appraisal of its acceptability and profitability or conviction to drop it, if goals are not being met.

Procrastinating about when to launch should also be discouraged.
We should deploy in phases. And findings must be written down for analysis. Running a successful business can be likened to a continuous twirling of the joystick of activities about the enterprise.
Strive to make the moves, smooth. You need continuous adjustments. It may not be easy.
Remember; *no venture, no gain!* And above all, be mindful of the brand image that your product projects to your current and prospective customers.

I recall the story of a - now popular - private hospital in my neighborhood. A good illustration of patience and focus. At its humble beginnings, it was derided. It was mostly attended by the people at the lowest rung of the economic ladder.

Today the story has changed, as the majority of the patients are now inclusive of the middle class.
Many big organizations and corporate bodies retain the hospital to care for their employees through referrals.
The two or three doctor-founders tested the waters despite the relatively more entrenched hospitals they met on ground. They started from a very small apartment space.

Errors were made, though not something to applaud. But they kept on getting smarter by handling only cases they had the proficiency for – that is, primary care cases. With time experienced specialists in the relevant areas of medicine have been coming around to consult there on days scheduled for them. They have bought many properties around them for expansion. An MBA holder was eventually made the Chief Executive Officer. The older competitors had to relocate elsewhere over time.

This further demonstrates that, it is not really about having a list of ideas that are shared around. But how we have identified and developed our own innovative ideas. Of course, this goes in tandem with a strategic focus to make our dreams come true. It will take time.
We all can have this list shared around in our hands, inclusive of our competitors. Ultimately it is about your passion, focus and your core skills.
To achieve greatness in your chosen ideas, you must nurture the humble beginnings while managing also the external influences. Do not let the noise in the market place create a permanent distraction for you.
With calculated patience, a well-defined vision, for your seed idea, will grow into a solid and well rooted tree of enterprise; this will bear sumptuous fruits into the future.

The Twists And Turns

Having put a finger on your idea… What follows?

It is the business development process – the twists and curves as I would call it. The idea must be in perpetual conversation with the target market. It is easier said than done as we can easily get carried away. Much attention should be given to changes in customers' tastes, trends, cycles and other external factors. The business ideas must fit in to avoid obsolescence.

You will also manage the inner workings of your business, that is, all that must be done to ensure a well-oiled business as a system. It is your identified comparative advantage – core skills and resources that will sustain the entrepreneurial energy.

As an entrepreneur, you will need to attend to the societal challenges. You will pick the coloration of these challenges you have the capacity to resolve. Mind you, you are different from the chap on the factory floor – hunched over the table, doing the rudimentary work. The chap on the factory floor, while his contribution is very important but it is limited in enterprise building.

Their worrying plate is what is physically in front of them – on their table. The entrepreneur bothers about these operational activities too, yet he must be about the vision and direction of the organization.

For new ideas to be accepted, they must be introduced gradually. Not at a single burst, like a *Formula 1* racing car. Human beings don't like too drastic a change in their lives, even if it is for their own good.

Creative ideas are best accepted, if they are released in phases and in little doses.

The company equally benefits, as it gives room for minor adjustments and fine tuning before the release of the complete package as envisaged. But don't let your competitor take a step ahead of you.

The hint you can take away, is that, your idea may not be conclusive when it is first brought to the market place. It is a journey. While mediocrity should not be saluted, it is equally true that you do not wait for perfection and perfect time. I am guilty of this too.
But after due diligence, just do it!

Chapter 5

Opportunities In K.I.S.S.

Not what do you think I am referring, which I have personally coined instead as… *"Keep It Simple Sensible"*. And not *"stupid"* as the last word.

My thoughts down the line might sound like a bit of bashing for some industries. Not at all. I am just revealing a space for business ideas and untapped opportunities - out of all the noise of technology in our world of today. Come with me…

Are we over laboring our senses because of the ubiquitous technologies that are there for the asking? Having over-featured products like array of toys for bored kids?
Higher retail prices are therefore asked to justify what some people don't need. And they get tied into the unneeded gizmos.
Some consumers are excited while some are not. There are opportunities for products for the latter. I am not saying we can't have smart features or gadgets that can make living much easier. No! But some products or services can really be over-featured!

Today, after technology has thrown many things at us and given us huge possibilities, I am convinced there is a significant segment of the market craving for simplicity – something lean. If the full featured smart phones we have today were first introduced many years back, they would probably have been too cumbersome to use.

In the same breadth, I still find it personally intimidating to use some phones I see around. Be assured I am not *"old school"*.

There is a very wealthy man in Nigeria whose cell phones are rudimentary as I have noticed. On it; no feature for the Internet. Therefore, no snooping on stored sensitive data because there are no such applications. I guess, this is a safer phone model for him.

In line with this, some people are not really excited about over-featured cars released into the market in the recent years - aside the unnecessary higher price tags.
Don't get me wrong, it is a matter of choice. I love beautiful things, but within acceptable reasons. These cars are not our living rooms, bedrooms - neither are they our office spaces, where we spend the greater number of our hours on a daily basis.
Anyway, I agree that the issue about cars is also an outward projection of our personality, the need for functionality and the psychological.
But how long do I need to stay in these vehicles beyond moving me from point A to B?

I could agree with features in products like a yacht, a boat house and the like. At least those ones could be stationed temporarily and used as an abode or office.
On the other hand, this makes me wonder when airlines emphasize the full reclining seats with claim of guaranteed and peaceful sleep, in their so-called "upgraded" compartments. They call that an innovative idea.
I guess it works for both parties since many customers are essentially irrational in their buying behavior. I have my own weakness too.

Anyway, I am wondering here; *"can someone really have a deep sleep – with good snoring in tow – outside his bedroom, many miles above in the sky?"*

It is a funny marketing gimmick that some people of affluence and other fringe customers get excited about. Anyway a shrewd business sense says; give the market what they want or seduce them into buying what they do not really need. That's selling.

I want to tell car and other gadget manufacturers, that there might be a huge market for less-featured products. It is my opinion there is still an appreciable market segment for minimalism.
Many still love less featured cars and gadgets built in. Car manufacturers and other gadget manufacturers should think about my free advice, if you are one, reading this.
Seriously, let them look out for those unique customers. I read somewhere about a young guy that got excited after locating and buying a mint fresh but retired *Nokia 3310* phone in Dubai, this 2016.

The *KISS* (*Keep-It-Simple-Sensible*...not stupid) consumers like me are waiting for some products to be toned down and of course the price reduction that goes with such. A different demographic, I must say – who are not necessarily old school are waiting.
Some of us just love some things served simple, effective and efficient. That will be a good innovative idea.

The population is aging in many countries, so some prospective older buyers may shy away from newer multi-featured products - even services. Not because such people can't afford them, but they are not ready to go through the steep learning curve of some widgets.
I know of a 29 year old young man, who bought his new laptop in 2016 but changed the operation systems to Windows XP, being an older version. He was used to the Windows XP. And he doesn't have much time to study and be tampering with the current version.
I repeat that I am not advocating that we should not move forward.

Some industries can now choose to create a new line of less featured products which can translate into additional income. Mr. *Warren Buffet* couldn't have been considered to be less smart using a relatively older car for years until the very recent, when he changed it.
Yet prices quickly shot up on *eBay* where his older car was put up for auction. The increase I presume could be for a different reason.
The lucky collector could become very rich, by owning it and having to sit on the same seat as the old man. I guess if the old man were to pick another car to drive, he would prefer less buttons and widgets. Those studs and buttons that could go hay wire in the middle of nowhere.

There was a time my car keyless remote just stopped working. It would scream intermittently. I tried everything and there was no relief.
I simply ignored it. I used the key…direct. Problem solved.
I just didn't have the time to bother even though I love the convenience of keyless entry. Few days after, surprisingly, it started working again.
It took me two years before I stumbled on the culprit in the rear booth. *Ah, ha*, I saw the controlling device there, when sealing some things. My car electrician could not discover what the cause was.

Despite the onslaught of technological ideas today, some people are still very frugal about the use of technological products. Some see them as an overload on their mental well-being.
Personally speaking, I have never used a blue-tooth ear-phone receiver because it is just too much for my wellbeing. I don't work with the CIA. Neither am I, *James Bond (007)* nor a *Robocop*. So I may not need it.
I had a sibling who told me he visited his doctor several times with a chronic nagging headache.
He narrated to me, that he was given many pills, yet he didn't get any relief. Suddenly, one day, he chose to remove his blue-tooth cell phone receiver from his ear. Within an hour and thereafter, he discovered his

weeks of headache eventually disappeared same day. That was the end of this particular device for him. He is a gadget freak though.

It is a free world; you have to make your choice. Look around you and keep tabs on the seductive tactics used by manufacturers, as they push newer versions and models of products into the market. If they were to be released as originally conceived, it might have been too overwhelming for an average user.
An idea is waiting there to be tapped by you.

Chapter 6

Ideas Worth Taming

The best business ideas are the ones you can create, develop and that can be tamed. While at that, you need to picture different scenarios as all ideas carry a measure of relative risk. Therefore you will need a clear state of mind before you deploy your energy and hard earned resources.

You should strive to have a backup plan, not if you can but you must. You cannot know if your idea will succeed or do otherwise in the first few months or longer.
But you have to get going to make it do well. It is easier said than done as we tend to exhibit this knee-jerk emotional reaction. This happens when we stumble upon ideas that appear as good prospects. There is a need to increase awareness because it is mentally hard to develop self-control. But we must try.

My advice is that the business you set out to do should be easy for you and your team. Pick ideas you are sure of or you can learn about easily, quickly and with improvement over time.
Then you as a founder can oversee even if you won't be directly involved in the daily grind.
Watch that team or partnership in whatever arrangement.

That reminds me about 11 years ago, I was appointed as a management consultant to a small outfit owned by a trusty client. However, I politely dropped out when the technical consultant – my partner - was trying to confuse me by not giving me adequate information.

I couldn't plan without having correct information to meet the client's set objectives. And the final responsibilities were on my shoulders to make profit for the business.

Not surprising, down the line, the technical partner – with the full control - suffocated that promising business for that client. Sadly, the business folded up in less than a year. I had left to protect my name and integrity. Thank Heavens.

In the course of time, as you get bitten by the entrepreneurial bug, you can push further to the riskier ventures, which ought to give higher returns. You will have to research the idea that consumers really need. Consider yourself lucky, if that idea is about what you are passionate about too.

That reminds me of the enterprising spirit of the lady entrepreneur, *Oprah Winfrey*. She simply loves to talk. Her millions of fans equally love to hear her talk to them. That brings her a lot of fortune and relevance; doing what she is naturally inclined to do.

Many may not be blessed like her. And many are still searching for what they are comfortable with. That is life. So discover your own business idea that is in sync with that market niche; that is willing to pay for your services or products.

On the other hand, if what you are passionate about is not yet appreciated by the market place, don't be discouraged. That's the reality of life.

What you do is to find out what other services or products people really want to pay for.

Pick the ones you can learn how to do very well. If the idea is well positioned as valuable in the eyes of the consumers, then you are in business.

Thereafter, you will naturally develop the passion for it with time, once you start seeing good money in your bank account. That non-existent passion would evolve, even if you did not have it earlier on.

In addition to the good income, you might derive additional benefits from seeing the joy in your satisfied consumers.

Seeing that joy on their faces could be invaluable to some entrepreneurs. That is not to rule out some naughty customers. If you are fed up with their tantrums, despite all your efforts to resolve their issues, gently settle them and avoid them. And move on. With good customer relationship, these ones are not in the majority, I promise. But be sure your company is not really the one at fault.

On the other hand, if you feel you are not really cut out to oversee a particular business idea, despite the good income. Go ahead and employ a competent hand to run it on your behalf.

You could choose to sell part of the ownership, for a wider supervision, aside your total direct control.

Selling part of the equity to others will bring in new capital. You will also get their greater commitment to managing the business. However, this must be well thought out. And there will always be time for everything. This is expected to translate into a solid business for the future. This is how to blossom your innocent seed idea to greater heights, quickly.

Having delegated the supervision to a board or team, you can then with a relaxed mind, choose to work as an employee in your own company.

But you must still remain as a member of the board. Free time would be available to do additional things elsewhere. These will be the things you are passionate about – maybe for your soul and not necessarily for the money.

Today, some multimillionaires – the founders - have gotten mentally tired of running their businesses as they did from scratch. The passion is there but the mental power has ebbed.

The energy is missing for the daily grind. Some of them have chosen to redefine their purpose in life. This clique has wisely brought – the very experienced but decent – people on board, while they pursue other private passions.

Can we say that of Sir *Richard Branson*, Mr. *Bill Gates* or Mr. *Warren Buffet*? Have they left their seed ideas they started from cradle to other people to help them manage?

I think they have, in a way. Not necessarily absolutely.

On the other hand, you will find others even at their retirement age, who still refuse to let go. They are still imbued with so much energy, yet they stick around for different reasons. Some derive much joy in that direct involvement of their now matured seed ideas till they pass on. It is their choice, if that makes them happy, let them continue. Why not?

Final thoughts:

Our deliberate connection with the societal needs would reveal so much, only if we are attuned. As courageous entrepreneurs abiding with faith, we should create a timeout from the rat race. This enables us to listen to ourselves and listen to our world. Ideas get thrown up this way but may not be the only way. We need to reserve some periods for self-reflection, to feel the real needs of our humanity and self.

We should make it a habit to nurture our soul, to see beyond what is readily obvious. The smart ideas may come as a spark or delayed over time. Entrepreneurs are to discover and solve our earthly challenges; to improve upon our human experience. It could be an individualistic or a team assignment. It is not about looking up a list of identified business ideas as suggested by others. Everybody knows about all these lists. Discover yours!

The different colorations of service delivery are waiting for the small business owner to pick from. You are the innovative middleman between a paying consumer and an idea that solves problems.
Such a list might be agreeable with you. But when you search deeply, you need to discover yours – with a different slant. The unique business opportunity leads are there to be found out, if one looks very-well.

After the exercise of due diligence of coming up with new ideas has been completed, it is possible you would have found a chest of profitable business opportunities to validate. But you must be mindful of time and season. These are the elements that may rock or capsize the boat of opportunities, making them obsolete, even before launching.

We are told, that the founders of *Twitter* were about to launch a different business idea until a stiffer competitor came into the field of play. They backed out and came up with Twitter instead. And better for it. Forget the lists and create yours. Use your resources and your understanding of the pains yearning for relief and improvement from the market to start something.
And above all beyond what anyone instructs, including me; be pragmatic, as always, in your unique situation.

PART TWO

Chapter 7

Define Your Market

Marketing Versus Selling

Let me quickly clarify the difference between marketing and selling as popularly defined in management studies. However, my goal is not to be too academic but to provide you with useful tips that you can put into practice immediately.

Anyway, in the formal study of business, marketing as a term is the broad umbrella. Selling is just one of the elements under it. Other elements would be product or idea development, pricing, advertising, promotion, public relations, merchandising and the entire gamut.

In our daily conversation, the word, "selling", is mostly used interchangeably with the word "marketing".

Also, you probably would have come across the term called, the "Marketing Mix" concept.
This consists of the 4 p's *(four "pees")*, which are **p**rice, **p**roduct, **p**lace and **p**romotion. They are just compartments to simplify overall marketing strategy. In some instances, these elements flow into each other and may not be fully delineated. For instance *"place"* would include the *"ambience"*, especially with service businesses – such as with professionals.

Another dimension of selling is this:
Beyond products and services, selling can also take place between two entities. In our human interactions, we all must sell ourselves to the other person, to achieve our aim. We may not be conscious of it but we do it, at every bat of an eyelid.

Having cleared that out of the way, let's move on...

Who Your Customers Are

You must identify that section of the market that is really, really hungry for what you have. However, your identified segment of the market must be deep enough, to guarantee long term demand of your service or product.

If the market is not deep enough at the outset, you must determine if the demand could increase in the future; maybe through rapid increase in population or changes in tastes and trend. Otherwise, the idea may not be marketable. Drop it, no matter how much you must have romanticized over that idea.

A market that lacks depth and is stagnant would not be a profitable venture for the long haul. You need to know those within the market place or public who are so much in need of your offer. That is your segment or niche waiting to be served; as they want it and they must be willing to pay your price.

You can't be all things to all people. Only few businesses on this planet are. As ubiquitous as *Microsoft, Facebook, YouTube* are, there are some smaller companies that provide unique services within the same industry. With the thousands of users in their own market segment, they make good recurring profits.

No wonder, some mum-and-dad's *"bed and breakfast"* that have existed in the same cosmopolitan city, with other five star hotels, still survive till today.

These services at both extremes still post profits, year in year out. These small companies got their marketing strategy right to remain in business. Though they may be approached for acquisition – at mouth watery offers - by the giants, if the latter feels threatened.

The market place is complex. Majority of consuming public naturally have an average taste and expectations.

There are also the pure non-conformist consumers yearning to be served.

You simply study their niche to determine, if their tastes are marketable, profitable and sustainable.It may not surprise marketers that, people with uncommon tastes in the society, do cut across the economic ladder.

The Demographics

Demographics as we used to know it amongst the human populace have changed. Beyondthe traditional ones, such as gender, height, age, family structure, disposable income and the rest, new groupings have evolved. When we reflect on them, we see possibilities waiting to be taken advantage of.

In marketing, positioning a business may not necessarily be skewed to any of the two extremes of serving the affluent or the poor.
Targeting multiple segments across the economic spectrum can be quite demanding for a new business. If that interests you, the best way to go, is doing it one after the other. And that can take a few years after mastering each segment.

Better still, the most rewarding segment falls in between, the so-called middle income group. Here, the market tends to be much deeper in population than the rich and tend to be more profitable over time. However, the state of the economic development of the country will have a big influence on your final decision.
What I am saying is that, determine the sector that guarantees a larger market, go in there and serve the consumers. The bigger the market segment, the bigger the demand now and in the future.

Do not rush into the very affluent market segment which tends to have limited population. Ensure the segment is deep enough, to give you an assurance of continued business, and profitability into the future.

For those itching to serve the exclusive rich clientele, you must have adequate resources. You must also realize that these sophisticated consumers are very, very discerning and can be difficult to satisfy most times. If your business decides to diversify into this segment, I will advice that you use a portion of your reserves to test the waters, first. You could scale up, if you meet success over time.

On the flip side of the coin, lower income buyers would give you little margins. If the market is deep and the product is quickly exhaustible, you may venture into it. But if the returns are not encouraging, veer off into another segment or business idea.

Let me take you through a few developmental thoughts, many marketers go through in research and development. As I have said elsewhere, managing a business is both a science and an art. Entrepreneurs do traverse both worlds. The world or the market place also bothers on some eccentricity. A formidable marketer, *aka*, entrepreneur must know how to tow that line.

As you can't be all things to every consumer. Concentrate on your strength. There are occasions, when just a few customers ask for an unpopular item. Note the frequency of such demands over time. Work out the cost-benefit to your business. If it is not going to give you a good return on your expenditure, in a timely manner, do not stock it. Simply tell your clients, you do not stock the unpopular items.

Years back, I remember we stocked up average priced optical frames in my eye clinic. Within our resources, we were able to maintain a reasonable large inventory, to care for many tastes. But not all tastes, a business can take care of. That won't be smart. With the variety we had, we were able to make our profit in a timely manner.
The cost at which we bought the frames from our suppliers – a few on credit - we could meet up with our obligations. We equally satisfied our suppliers and patients.
But I realized a few patients, in the tiny minority, were asking for the very expensive designer frames. I was tempted to stock up on credit, from our

supplier to meet this demand. But we couldn't be too sure, of the frequency of future demands.

The question I asked myself, was; *"would the business support the unused inventory, if this class of patients seldom patronize us?"*
Other clinics had positioned themselves to serve that segment. The business was positioned to serve the middle of the road, economic bracket. Out of curiosity, few costly frames were stocked up. Not surprising that, onlya few were eventually bought over time.
The remainder was sold off at heavy discount, just to recover our cost. We paid off the supplier after that. We realized we had to concentrate on our initial strategy; that is middle-range priced frames that sold well.

The lesson; if your business does not have the resources to handle some infrequent requests, let such requests from customers go for now. When the business is endowed in future, you may look at them again, if they could be financially feasible. A polite explanation to clients of possible future consideration would be made known to them.

Do not promise or stress yourself too much, on what the business cannot give, at a moment.
You may stock up when you have observed the request is becoming more with demand. If the item is not too costly, then you can buy one or two to see how it goes in terms of demand.However, if the items would disrupt your sacred cashflow flow, please concentrate on popular tastes.

Let us look at another scenario. Assume you are a lawyer, who specializes in certain aspects of the law.
If you are approached to handle other types of briefs repeatedly, because of your honesty, brilliance or dedication, you may set up a small unit to see how it goes. By choice, the firm could ignore the extraneous request, if it wouldn't give it the best shot, as always.
Simply thank the clients, and refer them to another competent firm. But one thing you could do is to leverage on this request.

When you organize your occasional promotional activities with your regular clients equally, invite those clients too with their friends and loved ones. New clients – your own type - may be amongst their loved ones. That's a big bonus for the business.

A business must be active rather than being reactive in the market place. A successful business takes the initiative on behalf of its consumers, to serve them better and more.
In the presence of adequate resources, care to listen to the market and deliver more. This can be considered, as long as the additional task would not jeopardize reputation or compromise competence.

We may not easily tell when the trend in the market place has changed. It creeps on businesses, unannounced, so watch out for them. It actually starts gradually, quietly without much noise. But the discerning entrepreneur is able to see the patterns. She sees the emerging order. A successful marketer must abide by the non-negotiable mantra of constant awareness of changes in market needs. Let's reflect on these thoughts.
If we ask; why do most people in the Northern hemisphere go for black colors or shades of grey, in their choice of fabrics and apparel?
Due to globalization, are we seeing more people with tastes, for bright colors in such places? How deep are these new demographics, if they exist at all?

These questions raise the need to look at the sensibility and uniqueness of a culture, in defining tastes and consumption patterns.

Assuming, if you were a manufacturer of umbrellas, would your white umbrella be in high demand in China, across the poor and the rich? No! Because, white rather than black, is for mourning in that place.

If your company were to be the sole custodian of the air – that we all humans must breathe - the market may not have a choice, but go with your dictates. This is an extreme example of a seller's market. There are few companies that enjoy this absolute monopoly in the world.

Could it be you have discovered the cure, to the most terrible diseases? The whole world is still not your oyster, because some people, by providence would still be in good health till old age. They wouldn't buy your product. Still, you will need to identify your market of the sick.

As I said before, *Microsoft* products, as ubiquitous as they are, still fight for a share of the market with *Apple* and its related products. Consumers will always have their preferences.Some authors still prefer to write on paper. Some relatively young people still prefer same. The pens, pencils and the rustling sheets are still their favorite. And that is a market segment that still exists up till today.

Chapter 8

Testing The Market

Why did the *New Coke* reported to have failed? Could it have been due to a lack of a thorough research?
Did they miss out anything worthwhile on the test marketing? I never can say - beyond the information released into the public domain. Big companies have their own best kept secrets. We are only told what they are legally obliged to say.
Test marketing is simply putting across your products – in a modest form or as a prototype – to get feedbacks from a segment of the society. You can do this for new products or an existing one where adjustments have been made. Aside the product make-upitself, you will be testing for other criteria.
One of the main goals is to find out about your assumption about the potential consumers – their behavioral pattern. You also want to know the adjustment to make to the product.
The feedbacks will also avail you whether you should go full throttle, modify yet again or abandon the idea. The timing of coming into the market may not be right.
There must be a checklist of criteria that must be investigated. Some pertinent questions would include the following:

What should be the best configuration of the product?
What price range would the potential consumers afford to pay?
How important is your offering to your target audience?
What is the position of the product-in their scale of preference in general consumption?

How will the product be produced and presented?
Is the market big enough to cater for you and other would-be competitors?
Is the market growing; will it sustain the long term growth of the business?
What is the frequency of demand within a day, month, a year or in the future?

These parameters cannot be exhausted here. They have to be tailored to your own market and business idea.
Getting this exercise done on a low key, still involves getting out of your zone of comfort. It will be a purposeful snooping around. Asking questions and getting responses to these questions.
Some answers will also be discovered, when you make inferences from relevant pieces of information, which could be found online and offline.

On a few occasions, when you catch entrepreneurs watching TV, most are actually looking for clues. These are clues about business opportunities, as well as to confirm an aspect of an ongoing informal research.
Research could also be by simple observation of your environment and beyond. You will write down your observations. And you start prioritizing them for a thorough analysis. Granted, there are people who are not given to figures and logical analysis. But these things must be done.

If you are considering a business idea, get somebody – at a modest fee - who is conversant with analysis, to help you out. To fine-tune the objectivity of what they reveal to you, I will suggest two more persons carry out the same analysis for you. So you can have extra options of reports. But it is something you can do on your own.

There are instances, when testing and fine-tuning might take almost a year, before completion. Yours doesn't have to be. It could be as short as a month. While thinking up ideas to test as I had mentioned before, I will always advise that the trick is to relax your mind and put yourself in your average customer's shoes.
Switch roles and imagine what they could be thinking. It is not about

what you think. Who cares? It is a secret that works. That makes it easier to tailor your offering, as it is foolhardy to think for them.

As a parent, walking through a mall, you will know what your different kids would appreciate, as a gift. Likewise, try to study your market.
You will be able to have more insight into their idiosyncrasies. Designing the field test would have been subjected to these assumptions. The feedback you get gives you more insight where you are wrong and right.

You'll also hear in some quarters that the market does not know what it wants. That may also be true in some cases. Anyway, above all, be conversant with the real needs of your market.
Be aware of consumers' autocracy. As an entrepreneur, you have to deal with these situations. All decisions throw up related risks though.
We have seen where a product based on a producer's love for an idea, was welcomed by the market, without any prior research or subsequent survey.
We have also seen a situation where millions of dollars have been expended on elaborate research and testing, yet the ultimate outcome was a woeful failure.
What all these tell us is that, business men cannot be absolutely sure of all the outcomes, of their efforts and decisions. But research helps better, it doesn't have to be elaborate in some cases.

A failed idea might be as a result of the following:

Your idea may be very good but the market place is not yet ready.

Your idea may not be practicable in the real world.

Your idea may be good but is not well marketed; the right consumers are yet to be aware.

Your idea may be fantastic but will do better in another environment, state or country.

Your idea has not taken into consideration, a silent aspect of the culture of a place.

And more other reasons...

Do not ignore certain unspoken sentiments or the under-currents of a location or some circumstances during your testing. There could be a little bit of arm twisting, not easily known before setting up, in a particular place and the industry.
Such may not be obvious to you immediately. Players in that industry or location may not naturally offer any initial assistance. You will have to dig deep to find out as much as you can.
So you could imagine, if you are about investing your life savings in a venture that has given encouraging test results. Be cautious to tread diligently. You can't afford any error of misjudgment beyond the obvious. A little bit of being paranoid is less of a regretthan being too *laissez-faire*. After all said and done, you will know you have done your best inspite of the outcomes of the implementation – good or not-so-good.

Assuming that, after the initial but an encouraging test result, some companies will give free samples to create further awareness. This gives more feedbacks. This technique may not be the right one for your product, if you can't afford the extra exercise and funding.

Some may enter the market at a reduced price – common with big companies. Upward adjustments are then made over time. The ultimate indices of measurement, may take some time to be appraised. When that is attained, they can now plan for the full launch. The picture has gotten clearer.
As a small business owner, the smartest way is to keep on asking more questions. That is, getting the feedback off the target customers.
Once you quickly understand the mindset of your average consumer, it becomes much easier to position and package the product.

Sometime ago, I had a Jigsaw-puzzle making machine. Nobody to my knowledge in my locale had this machine, I guessed. I procured it without any research, to make customized puzzle units for sale. I bought the machine influenced out of my childhood nostalgia.
I produced the breast-pocket size units that carried inspirational content. I introduced them to all age groups, including adults because of the motivational content.
It failed. It did not fly!

We discovered it was not a product for everybody, which we suspected initially. It was only acceptable by kids and even at that, they preferred a larger sized format. Luckily lessons learnt.
Subsequently, instead, in large formats sales were made to kids. Knowing the core consumers is of the essence which ensures efficiency.

At the onset, it might be a marketing strategy to sell products that yield little profits or at acceptable losses. Such sales could go on in anticipation of bigger profits. Your circumstance would determine your reasons. Selling could be a seductive game, as it is in most cases. Consumers can be very stubborn. Some don't even know what is good for them. Even selling ideas to big corporate bodies - the entrenched bureaucracy can make them blind and sluggish.

More interesting still, when you offer a free trial, many won't budge until a competitor eventually comes into the horizon. And then it might be too late. So small companies can just go ahead and do their own thing but watch out still for the behemoths, when choose to wake up in your industry.

Business moves can be likened to a game of chess, where a more valuable piece than a pawn could be sacrificed, to keep the king safe. If that wouldmake you win the game at the end of the day.

Pricing Can Be Romantic

Pricing may be regarded as the weakest link in the marketing chain. This is simply because it tends to be more of an emotional thing – it connotes a perceived value in the eyes of peculiar consumers.

Depending on the industry, the retail prices may be scrutinized so much by consumers, while elsewhere, a low retail price may be misconstrued as of low quality. A basic retail price is arrived at, when you add the production cost to your chosen markup. That appears as a simple formula but in many cases it is not as straightforward.
The positioning of your product within the industry and the targeted consumer-type are some of the elements you will put into consideration. And there are many others too.

You will also realize that some products are not price elastic, that is, the price cannot be increased, beyond a certain point.
If you choose to increase the price, add a complimentary product, provided the extra cost of the additional item is insignificant. And again, the extra product must be valuable in the eyes of the consumers. An intangible service may go with a complimentary physical product and vice versa.

Let's assume you sell fish and chips, why not add a small portion of salad or a bottle of soda drink. Then jack up the price slightly. If you happen to be a car dealer, a free service for a year would be a good idea.

A plastic surgeon that operates on obese people may author a book on obesity prevention. Or have an exclusive membership weight loss gym manned by a trainer. Above all, ensure you had done your overall costing and know your estimated income.

Chapter 9

Don't Wink In The Dark

We read from the holy book that says; one should not put his light under the bushel because, nobody would see the light. That action is an indication of a wasted effort!
In like manner, in advertising parlance, it is also said that, "you can't wink in the dark". Because nobody will know, when you do so.

Therefore, a business that wants to sell its product but aims for survival as well, must be simply be noticed or known by its consuming public. At the same time, the market place has a short attention span. Brand loyalty in a competitive industry can also change.

No wonder big companies like Coca-Cola – which is over a century in age – always remind its consumers, in myriad of ways, of its presence. You can't just be arrogant or ignorant about advertising. How much more a young business, that is fighting for the heart of its target market.

Getting The First Clients
We are told that, an average prospect goes through a mental process, when she contemplates an advertising message.

This is the AIDA process:
It connotes the sequence; **a**ttention, **i**nterest, **d**esire and **a**ction – in that order. It is said a purchase isonly made when the process has been completed in the mind of the prospect. So far so good, it is tenable but

nothing actually absolute when it comes to human behavior and circumstances. But AIDA is a good guideline you may reflect upon.

Now, how do you inform your market segment about your product? How do you do this?
As a starter, you may sensitize demand, prior to the full product launch. Little funds can be deployed to do this, before you open shop. There are different methods of reaching the target audience. You will need to utilize the most appropriate channel of communications, subject to available funds. Creativity and boldness come in, here.

If you are not predisposed to really canvassing like me, pay a team to do it. *I like to work behind the scene.* Get your clear message with differential information across to your market segment. Go after your main segment. Go for the bull's eye - even if the population is lesser – as the whole world won't beinterested in your product.

If you have discovered the awaited cure for cancer you must still tell somebody. You must cure at least one sick person. If you are the shy scientist; tell at least one person of your new antidote to the dreaded disease. Thewildfire of the good news is expected to spread from that classical word of mouth. If nobody knows, the cure stays with you. And that will be unfair to your essence and to humanity.

The classical word of mouth could do the rest of spreading the good news. This approach takes time though. Other sales and marketing techniques however create faster awareness.

Another important point in selling which many business owners are not privy of, is the need to tell a brief but compelling story. A true story on how the product came about. How it is crafted and what it will do for the consumers. This is the background secret, why some customers easily switch to another brand that gives more insight. Be transparent and explain what they are paying for and what you do differently.

Many businesses do not want to tell much, about how their products came about. Think about yourself. Who would you trust the more, in a new relationship?
The person that tells you much about his person or the one who chooses not to open up, thinking he or she is smarter? I am not saying that companies must divulge the very sensitive information.
Not at all. That will be foolhardy. But apply tact and wisdom.

Getting new clients is better done, this way. It is a lot of work but you have to do it. The market today is quite circumspect. Tell them what and how you came about your claims since you want to exchange these for their money. This is the new thinking.

When a business has commenced, all appropriate ethical tactics must be deployed, both offline and online to reach target customers, wherever they cluster in very large numbers.
Depending on the resource at hand and the level of the business, different creative methods can be used. You could go out of your way to strike alliances, with already established businesses, that serve other products within your niche. However the arrangement has to be mutual and financially rewarding to both parties. Otherwise many won't listen to you.

The companies you approach must portray the same image you desire to project to your target.
They expect same from you. If you don't have the energy or lack the time, outsource the exercise out. Then find a way of measuring the efforts, for post analysis. This helps to fine-tune further actions.

In this arrangement, a flyer may be embedded with a coupon number; this is just an example to track advertising efforts through this channel.

This may not be appropriate for your business.

Advertising is a demanding exercise, especially these days when consumers have seen them all.

Today an average consumer is skeptical. Their senses are daily bombarded with so many overloads of claims, information and promises by salespeople.
To make a way for your service, it is a game of getting the numbers. Creative ways must be developed to strike a chord within a large number of prospects.
This is where the challenge is; for both consumers and producers today. Therefore a different selling tactic must be developed, that is believable by your target consumers.

Direct Marketing

A popular technique is through direct marketing, which can be tough. The return rate can be very, very discouraging. The overall product idea must be speaking something different and of value to your segment.
The product idea must make a unique selling proposition, different from other players. Your products may not succeed, if it is positioned to serve all tastes. Concentrate on one or just a few tastes of consumers. Let that boldly be delivered in your communication messages.

In direct marketing, let's assume the use of flyers or letters. Out of about 3000 sent out, you may get about 30 responses.
This 1% figure may be regarded as worthwhile, in direct marketing. Therefore you will need to reach out to a large number of prospects to get an appreciable response.
As discouraging as this is, in getting new clients, this is one of the reasons why your current clients must be well served, for repeat business.
Leverage on your good customer relationship and simply ask them to tell others about your company. Make it easy for them in these referrals.

Entice or give them a simple informational package that they can hand over to other people.

It is a well worn cliché that says getting a new client costs much. In that respect, a business needs to determine the future value of clients. Find ways of nurturing the relationship, by bringing their attention, to other appropriate goods and services.
Capitalize on the established trust. You do not treat your customers, as a one-off thing. As I have explained, it costs much to get one. People love being loved and recognized. How much more; customers that can easily switch to other brands? Put a system in place, to sound them out for life.

A Smart Way To Get Customers

Earned customers with a dose of patience is the future of customer acquisition. You will need creativity, money and continuous engagement. For instance, getting new clients can be done through a good email list. It gives a much better response rate than sending physical letters.

The latter has its own use, I must say. But find a way of not spamming people when you go the email option. And there is a way to go about this.
To work around this, prospects on that list must have been expecting information from your business. Prior to that you must have seduced them to signup for some tangible-little-gifts, to capture their emails. And thereafter you will communicate with them over time with useful content. So you are no longer a stranger to them.

In a subtle manner you ask them to invite their friends to get some little incentives. You can be as creative as you can use this method. It takes time.
For people to be aware of your website, you may have to advertise on Google and other news media; with an alluring but honestmessage. This is the fastest way rather than waiting for your website to hit Google's first

page when people search for your supposedly keywords. That is becoming difficult as a huge number of people are doing the same thing. It worked in the past.

Get some money to advertise and earn your prospects for your email. Outside the Internet let people know about website and physical address and what you do. In the real world, buy your target audience's attention and keep their mobile phone numbers and physical addresses. Entice them with something worthwhile.

Beyond the initial items you will sell to them, the real money comes from just any additional products you would sell later. Most will buy, because there has been a trusty and nurtured relationship.

Why Promotion?

Valuable promotional offers must be done on a periodical basis. This is to increase patronage by current and prospective customers. You could use the tactic to get rid of old stocks. The money expended must give positive returns to the business, otherwise, there is no point doing this. Every promotional activity is done based on a particular goal. Decide whether you will deploy at low or high season.

Above all, a promotional exercise may not be a guarantee of a successful outcome, if your products are of low quality. For small businesses, the promotional techniques are more effective, at the initial stage, rather than the much expensive advertisement campaign.

Promotion is also done mostly during the period of low demands to stimulate sales. Various packages are put together and some alliances are made with related companies. The joint venture would easily give a high inertia to your products or services. Discounts are given within a time frame.

Special reductions in prices for a bundle purchase are introduced.

Numbered coupons are given out for future purchase. The ideas are endless. They just must be valuable in the eyes of your prospects.
When your business has low sales, this is the period to reach out to your old customers with new offers, at a discount that they won't get at other times. Make it time bound and do not shift the date, even if they show up after. But revert back to your normal level of operations after the promotion period. When next there is a lull in the business, inform them about this opportunity; the response should turn into profit for you.

You could offer a free service within a time frame. You could offer a service, at a lower selling price than the prevailing market price. However, be careful. Low prices can be suspicious too.
At onset of a product launch, most big multinationals – with their deep pocket - use this approach to entice customers. However, prices are raised over time. This particular approach should be joined with other multiple forms of publicity. As much as you can, each marketing effort must be measurable. And I advise you keep records and test only one element at a time. This allows you to know the most cost effective techniques.

Public Relations

Public relations activities are routinely carried out, once the business has stabilized. The company's budget would influence the choice and level of activity. Publicity is an indirect way of informing the public about the product and the company. Most common practice is to sponsor events, where the potential customers would be found.

PR can also come in a different shape and guise. It can be used to correct some wrong or misplaced perception by the public in periods of crisis. You have to clarify and provide a smart explanation. But be truthful.
It is less painful on the long run. You can't fool people forever.

When it comes to selling your product, find out a means of measuring future patronage, as a result of these activities you have carried out.

Has there been a good ROI, (that is, return-on-investment)?

Sponsoring or organizing shows are popular PR activities. There are many other inventive ideasof human interest, which you can come up with. PR activities establish a rapport all the time, with current clients and potential ones. In the consumer's mind, they perceive the business beyond the tangible products being offered. Your business gives them a total and identifiable experience, despite competition.

Think like a psychologist, seriously speaking. Do not dwell too much on your expertise or skill. Your skill however, may be the minimum expectation anyway.

Assuming you run a winery business, which is a very competitive industry. Keep some funds aside. Get across to your distributors. Roll out a yearly wine-tasting and entertaining event. Invite selected customers based on some criteria. Let them come with a few loved ones, who would be possible prospects. Capture the new data of the new prospects. Entice these new ones and old customers with some offers in a seductive manner.

You can't be confrontational in selling to consumers. People would normally resist. Do not forget to revise and edit the cost of this campaign versus marginal profits, after a period. Six months, or a year down the line.

A marketer must always take the initiative. I personally failed on this, years ago. I did not do much. It is not a smart thing, being reactive in your selling or engaging your clients.
You can't wait for things to happen since customers have many distracting activities and their circumstance may change – where your service could be needed, only if you are still within their radar.

You must keep on stoking the fire of the entrepreneurial activities, doing whatever to reach out to consumers and more consumers.

Experiential Marketing

How do we reach out in the presence of all the noise, claims and persuasion unleashed on consumers, these days?

Today, the answer is;
let the consumers decide, how they want to be sold to. Marketers have adopted different approaches to get the attention of today's skeptical customers.
Because of this, a new philosophy in marketing can now be added to your other strategies.
This is called experiential or event marketing.

If a small business is keen on using this avenue, it will need a modest capital. Where feasible in some industries, the fallouts are very positive for the product.
The exercise entails the initial rapport with prospects, towards solving a basic problem. Products are brought to the prospective consumers for trials, at no charge or they are heavily discounted. There is always a need for a location for this interaction to take place. It could be in a public space or a private building. A semblance of it could also be online.

The initial objective is that you want to establish trust about the essence of the product. You want them to engage with the new product. You want them to ask questions and scrutinize the products. You also want to encourage feedbacks.

This valuable feedback is an opportunity for the marketer to adjust all the factors about the product before full launch. Patronage and better customer experience is most likely assured, after this exercise. In due course, when trust has been established, it is expected that they would buy. Subsequently after your subtle sales pitch, they are ready to be sold to. No surprises. The initial risk of the exercise had been on your part.

The Art Of Selling

Selling may start before a product is fully launched but it must continue throughout the life cycle of the business. Its outcome must be measurable, though this can be difficult, depending on the type of advert campaign deployed. Figures give a clear insight into how and what to do next. You are looking for the best channel to optimize the advertising budget.

However, there is the popular saying, that you may not know the quantum percentage of advertising, responsible for your future sales. Some claim a figure of 50% of the cost deployed. How do you measure the success rate?

There are several ways to determine the rate of success of a campaign. I will generally say, find a methodology, which allows the tagging of all the activities involved. Be aware, not all can be tagged. Tagging allows tracking and analysis of data gotten from the field. For example, put a serial number on coupons sent out and also find means of getting to know, who responds to what.

Selling ought to be done at least once a day. This may be through the Internet, offline or both. There must be efforts to reach out to the immediate neighborhood. You may need to hit the road, to do some canvassing. Discover and pursue other non-traditional methods to reach your market segment. Every competitor is using the same method. Be different by adding more routes.

As humans, most of us do not like to traverse, the least travelled or unpopular paths. Possibly it will be rewarding to find other novel ways, to say hello to the target consumers. Try the new tactics first, in stages, before you conclude if they will work or not.

When one brainstorms with the team, these uncommon channels can also be revealed. It is noteworthy to realize that employing the tactics from a different industry, could be very revealing and rewarding.

That brings a fresh insight to your industry. Clients' experience would be changed for the better.

Brainstorming throws up the possibilities in the mind's eye. You may choose to go under the radar to do your marketing. Before the competition knows what has hit them, your business would have secured a solid rapport with new consumers.

Selling may be tiring but the long term reward is worth it. If you need help, use external hands to do the field's job and ensure they have actually done it. There must be physical proofs that are verifiable.

In many countries, the availability and affordability of the internet has made marketing much easier. It depends on what you are marketing, anyway.

Also, don't forget to use the mobile phone as a marketing platform. Send bulk small-message-services (*the sms*). You can entice them with a token gift to bring them over to your service or store. This route delivers information in real time. They will link through the message to your website, where more details are given.

There are other applications that are churned out daily, to market to cell phone owners. Because of its immediacy, it is a powerful channel of selling. Be sure the sms messages are sent to the appropriate prospects. Buy the right list or clean them up. You don't want to market ladies hats to a list of gentlemen's phone numbers.

A list can also be rented from non-competitive businesses serving your demographics. The introduction can be done on your behalf to their clients, then, you can continue your relationship from there. Compensation has to be made for this service. You will discuss what is the best reward the other company is comfortable with.

Consumers are more discerning today. Always keep all data about your clients. Routinely get across to them to find out, how they can be served better. Ask them what they enjoy about your services, their criticism and their expectations.

The philosophy of building a customer experience should not only dwell on the product. Every marketer sells its product or offer the same service. But customer experience tends to differ. It's a good tool to differentiate in a highly competitive industry.

You may run a barbing salon, where tea or cappuccino is served as complimentary. If your competitor does same, find something more creative to add, which will entice your clients. Most consumers would only pay, to satisfy a deep-seated emotional need. And there mustn't be a depleted customer experience. Period!

Branding Beyond The Logo

Branding goes beyond the fanciful name or logo which many people tend to mixup.

Branding is the imagery a product projects in people's mind, most especially the targeted consumers. When a product or service going by a name, has succeeded very well in the eyes of consumers, there is that temptation to use its name, to brand another product.

This approach is called brand extension. Experience has shown that, it could work and it may not work. You have to test the psychological acceptance of it.

Extending a highly regarded brand name to other products is preferred by some organizations. And some make a good success of it. The Virgin brand, by Sir *Richard Branson's* businesses is a good example, like a few others. I think the stretching of the *"Virgin"* brand name, has succeeded to a large extent, due to the interesting personality of the founder.

On the other hand, can we imagine calling a restaurant, the Rolls Royce Restaurant? That may not stimulate your appetite. The eatery may lose some patronage. There are authors, doctors, journalists whose names are now like brands. Some have become generic in some way.
Within the *CNN* stable - the American Cable Network - you have programs named after some staff, such as *Christiane Amanpour* and *Wolf Blitzer*. Same applies at some other networks and industries.

On the flip side of the coin, there are also some infamous – notorious - names of people or products that have become popular. I recall few years back, when an outfit wanted to use an infamous second war logo, to brand its outfit to gain attention. That raised so much dust across the world. I would not want to mention the name of this symbol. I must respect a people's sensitivity. In essence there is much that can be interpreted in the concept of branding.

Chapter 10

Surviving The Competition

Competition can be managed from within and outside an enterprise. Amongst many ways of reducing competition, is by extending an extra benefit, to customers beyond their expectation.
Hearing about the word, competition can discourage some people from going into business. Competition would come. It is a reality you can't shy away from. To survive, you need to differentiate your product offering from others, as well as how your business is perceived.

I will describe a few ways competition can be mitigated.

Let's look at your offering different packages of same product at different prices. This might depend on the kind of product. This may be in three categories, ranging from the lower end, the premium version and in between, at both ends. Each category of pricing demands a different strategy and tactics to appeal to your niche.

If your business can afford it, you may position another branch of your business, within your geographical location, but should not be too close to the parent office. The additional outlet is not expected to be a second fiddle in terms of quality services. The main aim is to deter an intending competitor from setting up shop there, in future.
Depending on how far, the additional branch is from the parent office, you have to watch out for self-cannibalization of patronage, when the second office comes on stream.

In prior planning, the projected combined profit of the two places would be compared to the likable loss of market share, if a single outfit were to contend with another competitor.
If at all a competitor eventually comes in, your current profit might be reduced. But your combined profit, at worst, would be constant, rather than dwindling.

Competitive pricing is another good way to reduce competition. It works much easier on the internet platform. Eventually, the right price would be arrived at. On the Internet, you will test different prices, since *e-commerce* is a form of direct marketing.

The company through its website can engage site visitors with phased prices, scheduled over a period. The traceable and measured feedbacks are used to arrive at appropriate pricing and product modifications. Offering services or products as bundle or combo, if they are complementary is another nice approach. It can also make you stand out.

Locking up the patronage of your clients to your offerings is another method of reducing competition. Many companies like *Apple* use different techniques. Apple has many useful applications, some of which are free or sold cheaply. Some can only be used on the platform of *Apple* products. This lock-up tactic is also common, with social clubs. Access to their modestly priced or free usage of facilities, are only available to fee paying registered members.

Other examples are found with manufacturer of office printers which will work, only with their own ink cartridges.
We see the same model replicated on the internet, where beyond the free versions given out, by application developers, a more robust version is released at a premium fee.

To entice your clients further, beyond your own product, you may go into partnership with another business. Such an alliance could give exclusive discounts, pre-negotiated, on behalf of your clients.

For instance a lawn-cutting business; a repeatable service like this can get clients locked into a simple yearly contract.
The attraction is to offer an overall discount, than if the services were to be charged only, when needed. This relationship may be nurtured further, if the service provider introduces complimentary services or products to the clients.

Making a choice to relocate from a highly competitive environment, could be a more rewarding decision. If there is not much differentiation amongst the other players, price reduction is always the tactic used.

At the new place you can charge a premium price. If you can afford it, you may choose to maintain your primary location, in addition to these new additional, outlet located elsewhere. Continuous observation of consumer behavior and the market place reveals how to serve the market place better. This is another antidote to minimize competition.

Be conscious of trends, life style, tastes especially for your niche and the general business space, even outside your industry.

There are cars and hotels in the world with new models being churned out. The thinking of these manufacturers and hoteliers is to be on the continuous look out; to serve consumers with unique but different tastes.

The same philosophy applies to the otherwise lowly products, so the products or services don't have to be exotic. It could be a one dollar service or product. Do you have a shoe buffer in your restaurant that is located in a dusty part of town?

While entrepreneurship may not be for everybody, since it requires a peculiar mindset. Competition should be seen as part of our natural existence. It will always be there, either in our personal lives or in our entrepreneurial efforts.
In our daily life, we humans compete with one another. And some of us would do better, than we ascribe ourselves to be. This can be extended to

the business world. Therefore, the fear of the competitive world ought not to be nurtured. The way out is to learn and also seek a mentor. An honest and experienced business consultant can be brought into give practical solutions, based on real experiences.

Striving to know the secrets and tricks played in your industry is very important. As information is power, your ignorance may cost you so much. It prevents you from maximizing the opportunities in an industry.

Let me share my ignorance for lack of due diligence, about a business I ventured into in 1994. It had to do with the supply of a major material, needed for that business. At the price I sourced over the years, I made good profit but I just discovered I could have sourced them at cheaper costs.
The implication was this; I could have sold more items, at a lower price. My production cost would have been much lower, despite higher profit. I discovered this oversight, just this 2014.
That was 20 years of ignorance!
I discovered I could have eliminated the two levels of middle men, in my supply chain.

This discovery was made during an accidental discussion with a colleague, as we talked about our industry. There is a need to always reach out the more, in your industry. I learnt it the hard way. This revelation has opened my eyes the more.
And I am excited to dig much deeper into the industry to partake, henceforth, in any of my undertakings, even if the business is turning good profit.
I want to know more of what is happening behind the *iron* curtain
(*Is there still anything like that?*).

The need to understand an industry better is one of the reasons some aspiring entrepreneurs seek employment first. And that must be a good idea in some industries, in my own reckoning. They understudy as employees, even if they have the starting capital. They would rather work in an organization, take a lowly salary, make their mistakes there and learn the ropes. After all said and done, they can venture out into the world of business whichwillnot be in absolute ignorance.

Clients do not like surprises. Improve or maintain constant customer experience. The operation manual checklist makes this much easier than guesswork. No singular item must be left out.
Consumers are not really interested in your business but in their self-centered feelings. If they receive a worse experience, they will leave. They don't care about you.
If they still hang around, it is because they are yet to find an alternative service that will satisfy their emotional craving. That is why, it very important to encourage clients to voice their experiences after service.
If they are not happy and they say so, the business is lucky, as adjustments can be made.
Most customers would reciprocate good or bad gestures. Such feedbacks could reveal another service that could give a competitive edge.
Provide channels that can allow anonymous feedback, to ensure objectivity. That will be a gold mine.

Do surveys to gauge customer's opinions and needs different from what you might think.
Do not be scared of negative comments, it is an indication they are still interested in your service, provided you take the corrections. It is not about the ego of the owner or the clout of the business. It is better to be late than sorry. Take note of the complaints and make amends, even at a small loss to your business.

Remember that getting new clients is more demanding than maintaining the current ones. The fraudulent customers and time wasters you will know.

Despite the cliché that says, *"The customer is king"*, find a way of dealing with bad customers, without staining your brand. There are ways of how you can respectfully ease them out. Experience shows some clients are bad people, just like bad organizations.

As an aside where practicable in your business, do not tie yourself down to a single supplier. Aspire to discover more sources, with quality products so that you can get the best prices. You will be able to sell more at reduced or premium prices to your clients, therefore make more sales.

Lastly, the major antidote against competition is to get to know your customers. Serve them better, while you pay some attention to what your competitors are doing and the industry.
I do not subscribe to the idea, as suggested in some quarters, that once you can satisfy the customers, you need not bother about what your competitors are doing. That is not being smart.
I don't share that school of thought, since you are not a monopolist. Even if you were, our world today, comes up with novel ideas, which could cause disruption in any industry. We are aware of business legacies of centuries that have become suddenly moribund.

Watch your customer and your industry. Watch your competitors but do not dwell on it though. But see it as an added protective measure for the business to survive into the future. Creative innovations and sustained communication with consumers are the best revenge against competition. Your competitors are watching you too. Therefore, leave your comfort zone, sniff around your competitors, once in a while. Speak to potential clients. Don't fall for that wrong ideology.

Chapter 11

Perception And Location

Perception

Let me share an experience with you about consumer behavior when it comes to perception. Way back in 1994 I had a relatively young outfit – an eye clinic. It was modestly furnished and positioned to meet the taste of its location. The consultation fee was quite affordable, just enough for that location, unlike the highbrow areas few miles up town.

Three months down the line, the owner of an eye practice – an accountant - in an expensive part of the city came rushing to me, for assistance.
Her senior Optometrist refused to come back to work after vacation. And there was a backlog of patients.
She wanted me to be chauffeured to her practice, to attend to these patients, two hours daily for a month, until she could hire another Optometrist. This clinic charged ten times my consultation fee. And she paid me well for my service anyway; as I used only my lunch time at my new place for this moonlighting.

At that practice, one particular day, I saw a patient who was resided close to my own clinic - going by the records on his case card in front of me. For a few seconds, after discovering this, I wondered in my mind, if this same guy would have gladly paid a higher fee at my practice, at the downtown location? I doubted.

It was possible he had seen my prominent signpost, at one time or the other. But he chose to drive all the way to another part of the city to get the "same" treatment. But I avoided the temptation to introduce myself, that I had my own practice around his home address.

That instructive encounter got me thinking…
It simply buttressed the fact that location, positioning and perception in the eyes of customers go a long way in many businesses.
That is indicative that most consumers would tend to pay for the actual product, plus other non-product experiences they can get from a seller. It could be the way your staff attends to your clients, with a smile. It could be the neatness and the smell of your restaurant.
Many of these elements are contributory to the success and failure of marketing. When you know them and do them right, such could translate into additional patronage and more money.

Personally speaking, I am spoilt for a courteous service anywhere; I want to spend my money at such a merchant's space. A slightly discounted outfit elsewhere - with rude customer service, would not impress me. Therefore as business owners, with consideration to the available resources, we must be deliberate in looking at these enabling factors of ensuring we have a profitable business in our hands.

To support this further. Could you imagine this scenario? An omelet prepared by the same chef, would command different attention and price at a downtown - one star - hotel. But it won't be treated the same way in a *Giorgio Armani's* -7 star- hotel in the UAE.
The hotel guests at the different locations would even report different tastes on their palate. This is very interesting and marketing in general would consider this, seriously. But there is a limit to how far this can be stretched. Imagine how much price discrepancies can go - with a bottle of water - at these two places, I have just mentioned. There can't be much of a difference in price.
The trick is all about perception and ignorance on the part of consumers.

Marketers use this as a leeway to create and project a semblance of scarcity and exclusivity. But there is a limit to how much we far this can be done.

Let's look at this yet another example. How would you perceive two lawyers who have sauntered into your space – at different occasions - to introduce their legal services? One is decked in a pinstriped, *Saville-Row* tailored suit. The other came in a *Tee* shirt and jeans. Who would you consider as a more brilliant lawyer – even before they open their mouth to speak about their competence?
That is a food for thought... *I will like to hear your comments.*

Location

The environment you want to establish your business must be well studied. You must also look around if you are located well enough, to serve a sizable population of your market segment. And watch out for possible new entrants, in future.

Are vital resources close-by? What about the requisite manpower?If the manpower and other resources are not available locally, your venture might run at a high cost. For instance, it might be expensive to pay, if the majority of your highly skilled staff comes across state lines, to get to work. You may need to search for competent hands close-by.

What about the culture of the locality? The physical space and your host community rubs on the image you projects. Not all businesses can be located just anywhere. There will always be an exception, if yours industry is unique in this sense. However, this is important if you desire to establish an office in far-flung places or countries, you are not conversant with. You must first find out within a locale, the things you must avoid or adjust in your operational or strategic plans.

Studying the choice of location is very important. As I write this, I am quietly investigating a particular location that I am about paying for.

I like the place for a new outlet for my business. But I must snoop around still, to confirm the suitability and why the previous tenant left, the building. The not-too close neighbors might give you an insight. Maybe three doors away.

Be conscious about the local politics and other sociological issues that play out in theplace. You don't want to be harangued later on when everything seems to be working well for the business.

No serious minded business changes an established premises or location anyhow. Whether you like it or not, some of these issues do play indirect roles, and can influence the fortune of some enterprises. One of the reasons why an established business owner must work towards having more than one stream of income - as a buffer - against any unexpected risk of loss of fortune. While you may not be the traditional lobbyist, at the corridors of power, be educated about political policies that have direct impact on business. These laws do affect the society and the enterprise.

Talking about local politics brings to mind, the arm wrestling tactics of underground warlords or power brokers. This I have mentioned about elsewhere. These are the infamous powerful blocs that may not be noticed readily. You must determine if your business and your own personality, can cope with their demands. In some places, these are the influencers, who control the local commerce. The local law enforcement agencies might turn a blind eye when these opportunities turn up. They can jeopardize your business efforts, ultimately.

This scenario, I have painted here, may not be applicable to some countries. How lucky they are!
Where this is a reality, I advice you dig deeper and identify any caucuses and come to your own final decision. These are the unseen overlords that could kill the business, before it grows beyond infancy. Some are economic caucuses. They can crash the price, after you have settled in.

And it will be sad if you have expended your emotional energy and other resources before you discover these clandestine overlords. If your type of business cannot cope, it might be too risky establishing at the locality. You look elsewhere.

Let me share my personal experience, about a location, which was not my desired location in the first place. Yet I still went ahead to set up shop. This was due to some reasons. I will explain.

In 1994, having worked as an employee, for about 10 years, I started my own business.
It was in a location I didn't really want to be. But I needed to break the waters of self-employment.

Another reason was that, it was a place that I could afford with my little capital. The location could only boast of a small target audience - it was not an expansive one for future growth.
I knew all along, but I had my plan from the first day on how to mitigate this. I started saving towards having an additional outlet, as a matter of urgency.
Good to say that came to pass.

At this first outlet, business was fair enough. I probably was skimming the broth of that neighborhood. Eighteen months down the line but not to my surprise, the sales dwindled. I had reached a saturation point of my ideal customers. The business was running at a loss. I was not alarmed.

The second plan was put in place. I got a bigger office, in a more befitting part of the city, located within the nexus of my preferred prospective clients. If I had not started with what was available, I would not have achieved my desire of starting a business of my own at all.

I started a new line of business in the first premise, more appropriate for the environment. The misplaced sentiments I had for some members of my staff, indirectly killed the big opportunity.

That is a useful story you will catch elsewhere in this book.

Let me ask you ask another question. How do you explain the non-existence of a type of business in a seemingly attractive location? Have you thought of that about your industry before? Anyway, be wary of such but confirm before you jump to a conclusion. Others in your industry may not necessarily be blind or they might just be missing an opportunity.

Keep greed aside but crosscheck and carry out due diligence of such a location. This brings to mind my former boss' error of judgment.
That was in 1986.
She already had two profitable outlets of her business. I was posted as an alternate staff with a colleague, to manage this new but third office. My boss was obviously attracted to the milling crowd.

A fair amount of money was expended on this third outlet, to put it to taste. All publicity stunts were done in this area, but nothing changed for the better. Sadly, six months down the line we barely could make any income. She had to close the place after nine months despite the heavy foot traffic in that neighborhood. It was not a goldmine as envisaged.

The mistake I deciphered at that time was the class of people that milled around that environment. The daily attraction of the crowd was for a different consumption and if at all our target audience was among them, they wouldn't patronize such a service in that environment.

The two older branches, with the head-office were adequately located and positioned for our potential clients. This newest but failed branch, despite its - much less - selling price of our products, its presence was incongruent with the need and expectation of the surrounding population.
So the choice of location matters when setting up a business is important. Location in some instances can portray a business, in a particular light, to

prospective customers as I have said before.

The last word...

If your business has done well, over the years, in a particular locality, plan towards buying the property or another across the road. If it's too big for your business, you could rent part of it out, later after making the purchase. Share it with some businesses that might compliment your services. That is an added bonus for you. You won't pay for that synergy.

PART THREE

Chapter 12

Managing The Most Delicate Asset

In the year, 2014 or so, out of compassion and wise business sense, the CEO of *Gravity Payments*, in the U.S., did the unthinkable.

As reported, the CEO, *Dan Price* slashed his annual salary, just for a year, from a million dollars to 70,000 dollars so that a larger number of his staff could earn a much higher pay. This was a benevolent act, one might say, but it is also a win-win situation.

Definitely, this is expected to increase the motivation of the workforce with attendant increase in profit for the company. From what I read, he was equally smart enough to have fallen back on in his savings - built up over the years - to be able to carry out this act of benevolence.

Managing Employee Relations

This should be the natural fallout when the business gets bigger. Responsibilities are carved out to individuals, so as to get things done more efficiently, since the founder cannot succeed alone.
There comes a point in time, when all the balls of activities can't be juggled by one man.
You will need all the help.

You will take your subordinates through the new tasks with the help of properly designed operation manuals. A small business owner might become lazy to write these operations manuals, as it happened to me in the past. However, I have discovered they are very important tools needed to eliminate clumsiness at the workplace.

Through delegation, authority rather than power – as the two are not the same thing - is passed on to subordinates by a superior. This transferred responsibility does not connote absolute power, as it is delegated at will by the superior.

However, the superior will let the guy do his job, in accordance with the written guidelines of operation. He will report to a superior or the owner when the task has been carried out.

As a pragmatic approach, at the onset, small businesses could employ people with the minimum skills allowable for the task. You will also seek self-motivated, passionate and trainable applicants for full employment. Their pay is much less than that of a highly skilled staff, who is already set in his ways from past and more established companies. This line of thought, however, may not apply to some well established companies due to their peculiar circumstances.

Outsourcing of jobs is also another form of delegation. In this case you give out certain assignments, tasks or production to a third party, in whatever guise that is available today.
Therefore, you have ample time and energy to concentrate on your core tasks. You cannot do everything if you want to achieve great success. I am yet to know of an average car manufacturing plant that produces all the items that go into making its brand of cars.
The same logic should be applied to businesses that want to do great things. But you will need to work out the cost implications, quality and consider other important details.

Delegation of duty could also be extended to temporary or project based assistants who come in when you need them. They could work as remote staff, only to come over when there is a job at hand.
A growing business will demand more detailed attention and need for faster speed of delivery. Introducing technology such as software applications might help out in the interim but there will be a time, delegating an aspect of the business will be more cost effective.

Managing Employees: As Art & Science
In formal business lexicon, this is called, the *Human Resources* management. The most delicate aspect of any business is we - the humans. It is gamble owners must continue to play during the hiring process and when employees are engaged. We are kept on our toes, managing the team to get the job done.

Employees are more important than the most sophisticated technologies; beyond the tools and business concepts.
Truly a supposedly well - trusted employee, due to an inappropriate act, might sack a century old institution in a second.
It is important, as we accept the frailty of the human nature - both the team and the founder –that nobody is immune to human errors.

We humans can also choose to be good.
We can choose to be excellent in our output too. It is a delicate balance, which cannot be left without observation, rules and continuous exchange of information.
A proper methodology therefore must be deployed to manage employees and we, the business owners or leaders.
And for any team or group of people to succeed, the influence of the quality of leadership must be entrenched where applicable, within any enterprise.

We know a business is the intermediary between services and the public in search for values. The business platform must be firm. The structure must be acceptable to the consumers. And the human beings who must ensure these expectations are met must be managed.
There are many examples where in the midst of the right personnel, some businesses have succeeded because of good leadership qualities at

the top. And on the flip side of the coin, it is possible to experience failure due bad management.

The psychology and the matured approach needed to manage a team go beyond the technical competence required of a leader. Ultimately as the business grows, a technically minded business owner may need outside professional help, in team management and recruitment exercise.
Mind you, employees can dribble around your naivety, unless you are experienced in the study of human nature and social psychology.
Develop interest in studying others go a long way to attain success.

Your Team Can Kill Your Enterprise!
In 2002, I was concerned about the unskillful nature of two staff members. So I wanted to introduce them to additional in-house trainings to acquire new skills - to bring them up to par.
My thinking was that, this would lead to increased salary for them, because I would need such skills in the future diversification of the business.

In my personal reckoning, assuming if I were any of one them, I would have jumped at the opportunity. Also I did not want to recruit from outside because I wanted to make the internal culture stronger; and to save me some headaches from the indoctrination process of new employees.
My sentimental thoughts resulted in a loss, it caused me money. I wrongly assumed these staffs flowed with my beneficial disposition.
I was simply wrong!
They pretended as if they were ready for the in-house training. I was not sure. I could absorb their salaries still. But I was ready to sacrifice to pay.

I employed a skilled staff to head the branch. He also had an additional job description, to train them over time. They were to understudy him.
I invested money into the new business located some miles from the primary office but in the same part of town.
The new guy resumed at work. Alas, what did I hear two days after? The new guy simply told me on phone that he would not be coming to the new office again.
I gently asked him why; he said the two old employees had just made life unbearable for him. He did not elaborate more. I decided to ask the two ladies about what really happened but I wasn't convinced about their explanations. I let the guy leave. He was simply intimidated.

Though my investment was modest. I was expecting the new business to generate money for re-investment, going by my usual strategy.
I changed my plans. I closed the business at that location after trying out other options. The business lost the inertia to take off properly. I was hugely discouraged. On their own accord the two employees eventually left. I went back to concentrate on my primary outfit.

In retrospect, what I should have done was this:
I should have found out what my old employees were interested in before concluding they would appreciate the training. If I discovered they were not excited about it, I should have terminated their appointment, within the terms of employment.

The newly recruited professional would have been joined by a new staff, with passion for that line of business. The new hands would have been appreciative of acquiring the additional skill – free of charge.
Everything would have started afresh. I simply ignored the fact that in human resources management, you have a job description which must be

matched with the right skill. It is never good on the business to persuade a worker to fit in.

The second error was that, I should have not have closed that business. I should have looked for another professional, even if it took a while; but not the one that left. If I went after him, he would have eventually taken me and the business for granted.

Another reason why I wanted additional staff to be trained was to prevent the skilled professional from feeling indispensable. A staff that cannot be made redundant is risky for any business.

A business should not be held to a ransom. It is very important to always have a backup plan for important job posts. You may save money towards the extra salary of another employee for this redundancy - if it is feasible.

Chapter 13

Hiring And Firing

Recruitment Can Be Tricky

There are many reasons of employing new hands to support a founder or business owner.
At a certain stage of the business or if you are the elderly type, the business would be more effective with additional help. But don't rush into it until you have worked out the cost-benefits, ok?

There will be a time you will be sloppy or slow in handling some aspects of your business. This is common when there is increase in demand of your services. A business may need to scale up and therefore new personnel will be needed.

Another reason is that the founder might lack in some skill, and once the financial opportunity comes, he employs the right staff to take care of that. Personally speaking, I struggle with engaging with clients and I presume, some people do it better than me. One has to admit this.

At this point, the question you will be asking is if you have the funds to employ your first employee. In very rare cases, you go out to borrow money to pay your first employee in anticipation of a boost in returns.

It is advised you put aside, between three to six months' salary for the incoming staff – possibly from the income.

'MUYIWA OSIFUYE

Prior to the recruitment exercise, you must have written down the type of personality, the job description and salary for that post. What you write down in expectation as a job description must not be vague. It must be clear and understood easily.

The job description must be objective; and not designed, having the personality of somebody you know at the back of your mind.
The reason why you don't personalize a job around an individual is that the individual can bring any behavior to that job post, thereby holding the business process to ransom.

And again, the individual may not know exactly what is expected of him and those that come after him. This creates tension and unnecessary blame on personnel who are at such duty posts.
It does not matter, if the business has a team of two. It is a wise thing to have these procedures written down. The written operations manual comes in useful, to guide future employees, irrespective of who they are.

When considering employing additional hands, the financial situation of the business will determine when one should do it. You will also decide if the business can do with a full or part-time employee. Even some big businesses, do what is known as a "call-out".
In this case, a service provider would do a job when needed and get paid, rather than having a permanent employee on the payroll, who may not have much to do on a daily basis.

For those above 50 years of age, I will advise you to pick a business idea where the income can pay some temporary staff or full time staff. This makes you more effective on your core skill and services. Running the business will be less stressful and enjoyable this way.

Hiring can be tricky. There should always be a written set of guidelines and procedures before proceeding with a recruitment exercise as I have said. This allows for objectivity and therefore it makes things faster and effective for the company.

If you are new in business and not really conversant with employee engagement matters, you may deliberately seek out an established business person, who may not necessarily be a competitor to help you out. Such could be a friend who is versed in such intricacies of human nature at the work place. Such helpers could join you at the interview panel. You compensate them as agreed. A second opinion may serve you better to pick the right candidate.

Though the final selection is yours to make, despite contributions from others. For instance, if yours were a startup, you will directly be spending many of your waking hours with your team. So engage those your instinct can work with, provided they have met the minimum requirements.

If the business has the means or there is lack of time, it may consider using the services of an honest competent recruitment agency- the head hunters.
Beyond their attractive skill for the job, your own feeling and aura must jell with your team.
This helps everybody's creativity and passion for the work.

Recently, I was fortunate, where I had a preliminary chat with a prospective employee. After an hour or so, I had a feeling he wouldn't come back for the formal interview.
At the initial talk, I was not sure myself, if I wanted him despite his having the attributes I wanted for the job post.

Yet, I scheduled a further interview the following day. He promised to come. But he helped me to make up my mind, since he did not show up. I presumed he sized me up and the job description, and felt that was not what he wanted.

You need to dig deep and find out what is the motivation of a prospective employee and the pastime of your staff. And you must be open enough to let them know clearly, what you expect of them!
We stay more hours at work than we do with our loved ones. Beyond the likable skill of an employee, we should consider if the aura of a prospective candidate, jells with the team or not.

At work, as a visionary, you are always thinking of the frontiers of opportunities. You may want to confirm if your ideas will be useful in the real world. Entrepreneurship being a lonely world, you need to bounce ideas out of your team.
If you have likable employees around, even if they are not experts in what you think is the next big breakthrough in the whole world, you may sample them out, for their opinion about your crazy ideas.

I do like bouncing some seed ideas from my team, even if the response I am getting from them is not convincing. They would be allowed to give reasons and I do enjoy this. I may consider them or not, but their responses do help me.

A grumpy guy in my space would kill my creativity; one can imagine if all the waking hours at work are spent with such a fellow or team, no matter their super skill.
Hiring can be tedious especially if you are busy on the operational aspects of the job. There is nothing wrong in going through an informal manner

to get an employee.

Sometime in 2015, I visited a bar of a small hotel, where I occasionally nurse myself with a solitary drink - when I choose to be alone.
I watched how a particular bar attendant related with the customers.
I was impressed. I knew he wasn't getting the best of salary. I wanted to dig deeper to know more about him.

This actually coincided with the time I was on the lookout through an informal way for a part-time sales guy- a foot soldier. I needed someone who was matured and serious. I wanted to test the possibility of a few set of ideas I was developing before a possible full launch.
When I had the opportunity, I quietly summoned him and I asked about his day-off and other relevant issues, when he came to my office.
The initial appraisal showed he was actually looking for this type of opportunity, to add to his regular job.
Now he eagerly awaits me to engage him in this ad-hoc service. And surely I would take him in, once the funding and other logistics have been put right. So in other words, you could recruit though an unusual or a non-traditional channel.

There is a saying in managing employees that says; *hire slowly but fire quickly*. It all depends. As you know, your team is an important asset in the wheel of progress. Therefore, be slow and painstaking, especially when hiring the permanent staff. For start-ups, the business is better off when it employs people with minimal qualification, with deep interest for the work. With time they can be trained to meet up, with the requirement of the job at hand.
The well-established professionals demand a high salary which a young company would struggle to pay over time. More so, the highly skilled professionals have been set in their ways, while working with bigger

companies and such, they may not be easily amenable to a young business.

However, matured businesses can handle most of the nuances of experienced professionals since they have the capacity to pay them. Though, there are some small businesses, which at onset and by the nature of the industry in which they operate must employ a few experienced professionals. Because that would be the only minimum requirement, to guarantee a good take off and the assurance of ultimate success.

Above all, in good measure, it is good to do a backgrounds security checkup of all staff, most especially those handling sensitive assignments and tasks. It must be stressed in the articles of engagements, the importance of accountability at every duty post.

Firing & Resignation

Firing is a subject many employers would rather shy away from. But it doesn't take much of an effort, for employees to *"fire"* their place of work or their employers for greener pastures!

Many are actually on the look out to fire you, at the least opportunity. Some of us don't want to terminate the services of a non-contributing employee because of some emotional and sentimental reasons. Another reason could be the difficulty of going through another recruitment process, to replace the employee.

When we realize that to a large extent, the survival of a business rests on the efficacy of the human asset, we cannot but put sentiments aside, to hire and fire whenever it is necessary.

As employees can choose to leave the organization without batting an eyelid for personal reasons and we can't stop them. Therefore, on the other side of the coin, we should ensure there is a sense of self-preservation for the enterprise.

If the enterprise shows any sign of misfortune, staff and even your consumers would eventually get a whiff of an emerging demise, they would eventually look elsewhere to satisfy their needs.

So if a staff has to be relieved, then that should be done within the labour laws and moral expectation.

Firing is actually the last stage after earlier corrections of a non-performing or errant employee. When all things are considered there must be a proper communication channel between management and staff to remove any ambiguity. The rules and expectations must be written down to avoid denials or claim of ignorance.

No matter the circumstance, employers should strive not to run down a staff in the presence of others and customers. A client may read you or the business wrongly, since they do not know what must have happened earlier on. I must confess it is a challenge to fight this knee-jerk tendency at some provocative moments.

But it is worth it, to be on guard against some difficult employees. Praises can be carried out as well but that should equally be well-managed in the presence of other employees. The staff that has erred should be shown where he has gone wrong. There must be a demand for improved performance after admitting his or her mistakes. Some simply need additionl trainings on the job to serve the organization well.

At the initial stage, you want to find out from a defaulting staff member, giving him or her the need for explanations. You may otherwise get a revelation you didn't think of - good or bad.

If you don't pry for the causes - as a business owner - you might be short changing yourself. Because another employee might come to that job and repeat the same behavior.

I am aware in some cultures; volunteering opinions to superiors vary widely. So a supervisor must understand the psychological and other restrictive factors at play.

When there is a repeated incompetence or misdemeanor after the third query, then this indicates a crucial period of permanent resolution.
You must determine when to initiate the process of disengaging such a staff.
Be aware your team watches how the management handles differences, rewards and discipline. A wrong or inconsistent decision will always send confusing signals to the team.
Where there are proper laid down rules of engagement, known to all, the management won't be described as witch hunting. What is good for the goose will be seen to be meted out to the gander.
Nobody teaches how to let go of any employee. Your peculiar situation would be instructive to guide an employer on the necessary steps to take - without fear or favor, for the survival of the business, which existence must be guarded.

There are many reasons why a staff needs to be eased out. You must ensure and confirm that the fault is not entirely that of the employee. There could be a need, to move an employee to another unit; and that could possibly solve the problem. And need for proper training too.

The employee could be going through emotional, domestic or personal challenges. Agreed you are neither a psychiatrist nor a psychologist, do get closer to your staff to see what could be done.
Years down the line, when a business has reached a matured state, the relevant officer in the human resources unit, would be able to manage

the employees relationship better than the founder.

After failed efforts and the staff can't meet up with the expectations at his duty post, the business may indirectly suffer. It is time to let him go. You would call the guy into your office and table your sequence of oral corrections, written queries, efforts to hear him out and proofs that the business would suffer and the reasons why he couldn't meet the set objectives. Therefore, he would need to be relieved of the job, so that the business can survive.

Plead the cause of the business and let him or her understand, that he or she would do far better elsewhere. And this is always the truth. Some people may be a wrong fit but not courageous enough to resign.

It is better for them to seek other jobs elsewhere that would match their skills and personality. Follow the contractual agreement of termination and benefits as known by both parties. Ask for the response of the staff which should be noted. And pay him off accordingly.

It is a painful exercise, but the survival of the business goes beyond the owners and the employees, in most cases.

I say this because, if the business collapses, nearly all the employees would leave, without batting an eye lid. I learned this, the hard way, at the early years of my entrepreneurship - in the course of managing people. I can never forget this reality.

For startups, that have a singular employee, it can be lonely when such staff just leaves. And you cannot hold such persons back.

Therefore, do not develop too much, an emotional attachment to your founding employees, which is common amongst young enterprises.

Having said so, remember to reward a committed staff. The one that has a tenacity of purpose, they are hard to discover but they are out there.

Those that took the risk to believe in your dreams, through thick and thin, until the business is able to stand on its two feet - soaring into profit.
Such staff should be well compensated. They are rare to come-by Founders should not develop selective dementia, at this phase of the business. It should be a win-win experience. We must show appreciation and be thankful to such fantastic employees.

Most of us, as human beings may not have the courage to be employers of labor, so those who diligently work with us ought to be well treated. At the same time, the laid-down rules known by all would prevent possible over-confidence by an employee we have shown much respect. So the note of objectivity must still be sounded always, so that any conscientious worker, do not get carried away by praises and rewards,

While considering the termination process; if it would affect production, you need to initiate the hiring process discreetly outside your company knowledge.
Have your shortlisted candidates on standby. Then bring in the newly employed staff, immediately after the old staff has left. You don't want the old and new to meet unless you can't avoid it. Everybody deserves to be respected.
To minimize the pains or disorientation of the business, especially due to the sudden departure of a key staff, you should ensure you have a backup staff, who can work in the same unit.
Such a staff is originally stationed in another unit but such can be also be moved, temporarily until there is a replacement.
Where applicable, there should be inter-departmental exchange of duties for some employees, beyond their portfolio or job description. This is practicable for some businesses.

If the job description is so sensitive, you work towards having a sinking fund, which will be used for the salary of another worker.
Paying for redundancy may save you from temporary and permanent losses in many ramifications of the business, when a key worker suddenly leaves a company.

Chapter 14

The Manuals Of Operations

For startups, documenting many of your activities is a must. It helps in planning and making references and inferences.
Documentation is part of building a business as a system.
This ensures it develops a life of its own, irrespective of who works in there and possibly in your absence. Ultimately that can also give you relative freedom over time as a founder.
At different job posts, the activities that are expected to be carried out must be written down, in the operations manual. No matter how humble it is. It is a powerful philosophy as I have discovered recently.

For a self employed - working without any staff - this may not be necessary if you are the only one in your employ. It is imperative we develop it once the business expands and adds its first staff.
We business promoters delay this exercise, as we tend to be lazy about sitting down to write this simple direction, as I will call it. But it is worthwhile on the long run.

Every new job designation must have its manual of operation. These manuals are introduced to new employees, during the orientation period. Staffs easily know what is expected of them, when they go through the manual.
During the recruitment or interview process, I advise some of these important details are made known to the prospective staff.

There is no need for surprises at both ends.
With time, an established staff may modify this directive under the guidance of the executive.
They must be so designed that, the activities are measurable.

Let's look at a simple manual of a customer service post.
A hypothetical one.
The checklist may go like this; using deliberately designed choice of phrases and words. This is very important for psychological reasons, to make it a rewarding experience.
A section of it could have statements like this:

Greet the customer in a pleasant way – in a well thought out preconceived given phrase.
Write down his full names, phone numbers, addresses etc
Get his email and ask him to dictate it to you and write it down.
Listen very well to understand what he is saying.
Write down as fast as possible about his needs or complaints in details.
Remind him to repeat if you didn't get him clearly.
Do not argue with him, but allow him to speak his mind.
Now plead with him, that you want to go over the information.
Tick each question and his answers to confirm that they are correct.
And let him know you will get back to him at a particular time.
Did you ask him the best time? Write it down.
Thank him.
(You may build your own well thought-out, sequenced checklist, as you deem fit)

Let me give another example.
You run a grocery store, where the staff must monitor the inventory of

items in stock. He must amongst other things, know at what point the stocks need to be replenished. He must know how to engage the various suppliers, to get the best terms of trade. He must know when to report to the grocery shop owner, important milestones.

The operations manual for this store might include a section like this:

Write the daily entries of all the items on display and in the inventory.
Determine the rate of how each item is sold, on a daily basis or any other time frame.
Check the store and determine how many days the inventory will serve the store.
Know the figure that triggers a need for re-ordering of the inventory.
Ensure supplier delivers in a particular maximum number of days.
Keep all entries on this paper or in the system for the auditor and manager's perusal.

(As I said before, make your own unique check list.)
Irrespective of the business, whether you are a dentist or a barber, it is imperative you design your basic but simple manual. The staff must use them to get the work done. These manuals must be updated as the need arises.

The Best Management Style
Of course in human relations, a style of leadership is not cast in stone. Being pragmatic and giving considerations to the unique situation in front of you, is the best way to go.
My personal orientation is to be fair to my employees. It is easier for me and I equally expect total dedication to duty. I can be so fascinated by such a staff who is open to me and tries to be entrepreneurial in focus, but such staffs are not common.
When you engage a staff, their perception of business is just to do the

operational tasks in front of them. Period.
If you dwell too much on asking them to think like a visionary, you will be wasting your time. That is your own job as a founder or the Chief Executive Officer.

If you are too hard on your team or too secretive about the company's operational affairs, you may not get the best from them. Of course, you will decide those things that shouldn't be divulged.
The iron-hand style, may erroneously construe they are isolated and just being used. Though different cultures and mannerism of the workforce across the world must be taken cognizance of. A diplomatic management style will take any leadership far, in the presence of well spelt out rules, expectations, rewards and punishment.

The management style should be well understood to avoid confusion. If the majority of the workforce are not pleased or see the management style as being inconsistent, they will surreptitiously find a way of paying the company back in a bad light.
I warned earlier. Shun nepotism. The fortune of the enterprise might be put into jeopardy. Don't initiate and spread bad blood, even though you have the ultimate power, and maybe authority.

At the same time; never put absolute trust on any employee no matter how conscientious or how long such an individual has worked with the organization. Always give a room for a *Simon Peter's* denial. We human-beings are very complicated and we can be influenced for good or bad at any time. A leader should also watch out for his or her own human frailty and vulnerability, at the work place.
You may be wondering about the best management style. It all depends on your unique circumstances. Some choose between the two extremes

of either an open-door policy or a closed one. Other leaders bestride the two extremes, utilizing the different shades between the two as the situation demands. I am saying, it is better not to be too absolute but safer to deploy the best option.

I repeat again; there are aspects of the business you ought not to keep away from the employees. And in some cases there are some that may be too sensitive, that should not be divulged to your staff, maybe for a particular period or not at all.
For many businesses inclusive of the small ones, it is advisable your team knows about the turnover, expenditures and how the profits are arrived at. Let them see the books.

The reason for this is simple. It creates transparency and trust. It also creates a sense of belonging. It helps the management, to sound convincing when financial issues and targets are being discussed. Overall, this helps the psyche. To a large extent – not all – it will improve commitment and performance. I agree, the transparent in-house culture could be challenging to handle when you look at the outcomes - both good and bad.

For instance, if any employee feels, he deserves more than what he is being paid, because he is privy to the robust finances of the company, such a worker should be pointed to the written contract of emoluments. And such individuals should be made to realize, that the business is a separate entity that must survive into the future come rain or shine. There are possible future challenges which the company would have to solve. The workforce is being paid for its contribution as agreed.
There is no favor shared by either of the two parties.
If there would be a need for a revision of the salary structure based on a

significant but steady performance of the business over a time, a reappraisal can be carried out. But the new salaries and emoluments brought to play must be cognizant of the unseen future, if the future projections could sustain the increments. Therefore, while it is good to make the employees happy, the company's fortune into the future must be very well studied.

When it comes to financial figures employees are involved with, you can't hide it from them for too long. They will haphazard an estimate and come up with their own conjectures which could be wrong. And this creates a negative mystery about the organization.
If there are trade secrets and formulas, non-disclosures, legal instruments, such are expected to be signed by the employee with the help of the company's lawyer, versed in that area of labor law.
Even at that, you never can tell about human nature as there is no guarantee on that. This is why managing some peculiar businesses demands more of intuition and being observant.

Employees should never be treated as slaves, because they are our fellow human beings. They are the assistants who help the enterprise to achieve its future objectives.
It has been proved scientifically that most employees if treated fairly well, they will return such positive gestures to the business. And the business most likely would blossom. It is a reality.
As nothing is absolute, there would be exception of ungrateful employees.
Your job is to identify them and ease them out gently without hesitation but within the ambit of the legal requirements.
If your business goes down, no employee will cry with you forever. That will be your headache.

'MUYIWA OSIFUYE

I can say that a million times because, I experienced everybody jumping ship. Your natural but survival instinct is to do all what it takes to protect your business.

Let it be said that protecting your business also means taking care of your employees. Having said that, do not allow any uncooperative employee capsize your boat in the turbulent sea of your entrepreneurial journey. Despite your transparent and equitable attitude, there will come a time a few unappreciative employees may choose to leave you in the cold when you need them most.

As you know the entrepreneurial journey is a topsy-turvy affair, even as you are expected to do better than "yesterday". No matter your ascendancy in sales, profit and clout, there would have been moments of peaks and troughs.

When you are just starting out and your business meets some unexpected storm, despite your pleading, such individuals would rather jump off. They won't exercise any patience to wait, till the waves wear out.

I personally have experienced instances in the past before I had the means to put up a back-up employee in place. On this particular day, my only employee walked up to me the second day after drawing her salary. Baring that she ignored the terms of disengagement, she simply told me she was stopping work. She told me that for months, she had been nursing episodes of stomach pains. A lie! And I knew.

Going by my past experience, I was not jolted. I saw it coming. I had earlier thought she was not going to stand by me till I resolved the problem the business was going through.

Thank goodness I ultimately resolved the problems after her departure. The business bounced back, painfully though.

Employees Matters

Employees are human beings like you and they are there to help you reach your goals. They are employed based on their areas of competence. Therefore, they should not be left to the whims and caprices of an employer. A business entity that expects profound growth in the future must not be too attached to the shortcomings of the leadership. When the business demands more knowledgeable people, they should be brought in. You do this once the business can afford their long term emoluments, in conjunction with the clearly projected financial gains. Every employer of labor should be able to designate the best employee to an appropriate task.

We are told that, the car manufacturer, Mr. *Henry Ford*, engaged the services of the best engineers, to get his vision realized. If you want your business to grow big as a successful entrepreneur, you have to develop the ability, to locate the needed manpower and compensate them beautifully. Compensations could be cash or in other intangible forms.

All things being equal, they will make huge but steady profit for your enterprise ultimately. You just take on the leadership role, with vision and guide your team. Develop a system that guarantees a feedback from the work done, without any restriction or fear of sabotage from them.

In the beginning, a young business may not be taken seriously, especially by the employees. The staffs watch how you run the business. Most of your team will still be romancing the idea of seeking the greener pasture. It is to be expected. Some would discreetly desire to be with a more established organization.

This is the phase where you must do all you can, to be firm on the ground, irrespective of how the employees perceive your vision. You cannot let anything take you away from that entrepreneurial goal.

From your estimation of future sales, pay what the business can afford and not what you feel the employee has convinced you to pay. Tell the truth at the interview stage.

It is better to pay regularly even if the salary is modest. Your business' financial health would determine when the pay needs to be increased.

During the interview process, do not get carried away with a prospective employee, who you feel is so good, prompting you to accept to pay a salary, higher than your initial projection.

Do not employ such an applicant as it would be risky because the business can default; a decision that would simply scatter your plans. You may engage him on a part time basis, if that augurs well with your business operations. Be sure, this intake will increase the fortune of the company.

Study the personality of potential applicants and consider a variety of behavior amongst them. I will advise that your team is of diverse interests and leanings. Outside being rude or indolent, staff with a common mannerism may turn into an ideological force and may want to control you and the business.

Team Commitment

At the recruitment exercise, the culture and philosophy of the enterprise must be made known to prospective employees. Recently, I interviewed a prospective staff where I mentioned, that television viewing was not part of our culture in the office, so we didn't have one in place.

His earlier smiling countenance changed after I made that statement. He told me his previous place of work allowed it. I told him it was a distraction by virtue of the peculiar nature of my workplace. We rounded up and I scheduled a second round of interview. Of course he did not come back. And the guy was quite skilled. But I couldn't change the culture that was appropriate and fruitful to our own kind of business because of an individual.

Ensure the staffs are well committed to the job. There will be a need for supervisors to go round, to smoothen out daily operations.
The operational procedures cannot be left entirely to the staff, without occasional checkup; otherwise many things that are going wrong would be hidden from the management or the owner.

Watch out for all the tricks, the old staff might be playing, to frustrate the new employees. Let there be a firm and clear cut position of the culture the organization stands for. Support this with continuous communication with the staff through different channels. The mantra of an organization should be well communicated both internally and externally. Watch out for any staffs, which choose to hold the business to a ransom, especially those who have specialized skills.

Big Companies & Team Management

A solo entrepreneur attends to all aspects of his business.
You will be the production person, you will interact with customers or clients, and you will clean your own office. You will keep different inventory and accounting books. You will source for clients, you will change the bulbs. You are practically a one-man army. All at the beginning. Lurking behind such a solo entrepreneur, one could hear him mutter to himself, how big businesses manage a large retinue of employees. It is somewhat simple.

They put up an objective human management system in place, which to a large extent is devoid of the sentiments of the founders.
Such businesses might have started small but there was a vision for growth. Therefore, in their evolving strategic plans and objectives, the human resources system had to be instituted and developed. However, this system must not be alienated from the overall strategic goals.
The human resources system must be measurable, both in terms of quality and quantity.

For instance, if there is repeated firing or resignation of staff, many reasons could be adduced to this. The management must find out why. It could be as a result of faulty recruitment methodology. Be aware that the interviewer and the interviewee are equally under examination in making the right choice. Across the table, either party could miss an opportunity or invite trouble. This could lead to a wrong selection of an applicant or wrong acceptance or a mismatched job.

The internal culture of the organization could be a reason for high staff turnover.
For example, if the turnover of staff is high in a particular department, it might be due to poor leadership quality or incompetence on the part of the head. It could also mean that the job description has not been properly designed, thereby confusing the workers.

Competition amongst the staff should be healthy but to build trust will always be a challenge; as office politics must be well managed. Internal politics must be reduced to the barest minimum.
It takes a long time for internal wrangling to come to the fore and businesses mostly suffer, if this is not detected on time.
Human beings cannot be programmed like robots, therefore their

feelings must be known.

Good interactions amongst colleagues could be stalled, because of subtle imposition of religious beliefs, a hint of racism and even bad hygiene. As insignificant as it might appear, body or mouth odor can affect interaction and indirectly affect the fortune of an organization. Same applies to lack of proper public etiquette.

Problems may arise in business because of the personality of the owner or the chief executive. We are simply human. Some business executives do not have the capacity to get results through others.
Bad leadership might spell doom for an otherwise successful enterprise if such executives take over.

There are modern tools used in human resources, objective as they may be, we should not ignore the important role intuition plays. A well intuitive recruiter helps in the final selection of an applicant during an interview. Your instinct could be faulty though, but it could also help you select the best candidate, provided the minimum requirements set by the objective tools have been met.

To play safe, let the applicant work for a trial period, maybe six months, before full confirmation. Always keep handy the shortlisted names of the candidates; you may need the second person on the list.

Chapter 15

Managing Yourself – The Boss

Your Business Will Change You
Circumstances do force us to become entrepreneurs and therefore, we have to exhibit the right personality and worldview. An entrepreneur is a different animal once he chooses to be one. It's about leadership. It's about responsibility. It is about being a team leader because eventually, it will be foolhardy as you grow, to think you can do everything alone and achieve effective results.

Some of the circumstances that force people into starting a business will include lack of job, loss of job, under employment, or mounting debt and more.
There are also challenges of repetitive financial obligations that refuse to go. Your salary is simply not enough. You may even find that you are very skilled but due to your age bracket, the labor market finds you unemployable.

For those who are naturally not inclined to be introverts and shy but have found themselves in the business world, there are ways to manage this personality if it will directly affect your business.
You can learn how to be outspoken about your business and do more. You don't have to be vulgar or become a nuisance.

On a personal note, I could be regarded to be on the quiet side but the business world changed me. I wasn't aware that I had been doing much talking. Someone close to me brought it to my attention during my interaction with a client, way back in 1994. That was survival.
My personality had changed a little! Although today, that has been tempered quite a lot as one gets older.

If you are a professional and you are aware it is difficult for you to do a sales job, quickly plan towards hiring an ad-hoc or permanent staff.

At the onset of a new enterprise, the health of a business owner is of paramount importance, even more than when you are in paid employment. As a starter, on a small scale, you will be doing both the mental and physical work alone, until the business grows when you could afford to employ assistants.

Imagine if you are invited to a dinner with many sumptuous dishes beckoning at your palate. You may not necessarily eat to your heart's delight, if you have to make a 5 hour drive –early dawn on the next day – to keep an appointment out of town.
Your trip might be truncated if you had too much to eat and drink, the previous night. You could have your stomach rumbling overnight, making you sick the following morning.
You wouldn't want to postpone your appointment. That will keep your new client waiting at the other end of town. You can't afford to lose a major contract that can go a long way in your finances for many months.

Time must be reserved to reflect and meditate on successes and mistakes made on the job and to plan on what to do next. The life of an entrepreneur is a continuous brain storming one. You are responsible for the next pay check for your employees, the growth of the business and lastly your own stipend, at the beginning.

When I talk about meditation, use whatever style your faith finds permissible or your own accepted ritual that goes with your spiritual conviction. This you must do because you cannot just be a moving vehicle without breaks, just rolling on without finding out what the shortest route to your destination should be.
Something must shift inside of you so that you can run a business profitable.
What should shift will include your unenviable habit, your excessive introversion and other negative interpersonal tendencies.
Because running an enterprise is about curiosity, it's about courage, it's about bearing pains and it is about reaching out to different human beings.
Mastering all these will assure your efforts of continuous reward in the future. Of course, when lack stares us in the face, when we are heavily dependent financially on others for survival, a new personality evolves. But it must be for good.

Other influencers around us are of significance in this creative journey. And don't let it surprise you, as close as these people might be to your "skin", they can make or mar your efforts.
As a matter of fact, your immediate inner circle of influence be it your spouse, other family members or some friends need to be re-assessed.

You must strike a balance to get their cooperation, if that could be possible. Not because they don't love you, but because some of them don't understand what entrepreneurship entails and they wonder you must be crazy. But they won't tell you…but you must win!

I advise you manage these relationships very well so that you won't be led astray or lose your self confidence of that initial, *"I can do it spirit"*, you had at the beginning.
You can't afford to run a regrettable business because of over bearing influence from your loved ones. Because without a focused mind in the midst of possible distractions, you may not meet your objectives and milestones.

I gathered about a radical approach, that you could sack your spouse if the continued relationship would put spanner in your wheel of progress. That may be true within reasonable circumstances.

I would suggest you manage relationships very well. Same is equally demanded at the workplace with your staff and your unpredictable clients. You would pull through with wisdom and adequate communication.

There are also occasions, where your loved ones, team members and clients may give you a solid advice towards solving a nagging problem. This may not be frequent but keep an ear on the ground. You will need all the help.

The Fear Of Decision Making

As the leader, the buck will stop at your table. Making up one's mind about resolving issues is one of the challenges you must develop with time. Making decisions will become second nature, whether you like it or not.
You will have to live with your successes and mistakes as a result of this.

'MUYIWA OSIFUYE

My quick advice:
Read and learn – through many sources - as much as you can about business leaders.
Learn about winners and losers in life.
Learn about the lowly and the mighty.
Learn about the hidden, frivolous, the prominent and didactic.
Find time to reflect as you will be making many hard decisions, which must be timely too.
You can't afford to be a victim of over stretched procrastination. And neither should you act on knee-jerk impulse.

This balancing act comes with consciousness and practice, when you follow the right hunch and logical reasoning. It is easier when you strive to be a student of many things - learning from others irrespective of their station in life or industry. Find out how certain problems are resolved elsewhere. Read a lot of different books as diversified as they could be on different topics under the sun.

A successful entrepreneur is that person with a disciplined mind which is imbued with that insatiable craving for new knowledge.

Your essence is an important asset. This inner resource must be finely tuned spiritually, mentally, emotionally and physically.
This is not to scare an aspirant into enterprise or for those who intend to head an enterprise. It is just that these attributes are very important and needed, whether you are the sole investor or you are reporting to investor-owners of a business.
It is usually a solitary world for a decision maker.
As the head or a manager of a going-concern, the buck stops at your table. So there are certain ways that you must behave or live your life.

You must ensure you have a balanced mind, to meet the objectives of the enterprise. It will get easier because when we are faced with challenges and expectations a serious minded person will adapt when it is very necessary.
Therefore it is a life of inner conviction. It is a life of having a quiet observation and the need to study our immediate surroundings.
This goes beyond your locale, as the broader global stage is also included. Today, it is a globalized world, where there is an ever increasing interconnectivity of activities, both good and bad. It is a world of continuous learning, beyond the university setting.

On your own you should show interest in human or social behavior. This will enable you to see patterns, opportunities, orders, the changing life style, tastes and above all global trends.
It is a world where your intuition must be honed and developed. Why? Because you may find out that, the known logical arithmetical solution of, *two plus two, may not be four at times*, figuratively speaking.

It is a world where you will behave like a sleuth. Successful leaders in your industry are actually doing likewise - studying the changes in the market place and outside of it.
Because the market place tends to change, you must not let your personality blind you from seeing it in a truthful and objective perspective.
You must not allow the concurrent situation of your enterprise prevent you from making the right decision. Therefore you must mix with different consumers' enclaves, suppliers and all the other stake holders in your business. This can be done through the internet or you can engage them in the real world.
You must devise your means of doing your own informal research, on a

particular aspect of your industry. These exercises can reveal immense advantages to your business.
They help in accurate decision making, which may take you away from your comfort zone but you will not regret it.

Occasionally things may not go as planned and this where your strength of character is utilized. Granted there is no super hero of an Entrepreneur. Accept that reality.
There is an element of luck - that is my observation even if some people refute this.
But you must still work hard and be smart in your approach.

Simply do not panic for too long, when you need to resolve crisis. This will be revealed towards the end of the book on how to handle this. It is a popular technique that works. It helps you to clear away all the cobwebs found in the most critical situations, in the business and your personal life.
There is no everlasting and perfect solution but to make informed judgments based on the circumstances at hand, to reduce failure to the barest minimum - and that is success defined.
For micro-businesses and the self employed, you will learn how to come your own conclusion.
It could be lonely, even your staff, spouse or friends may not know your pains. Though it is much easier you discover an honest person, to share your mind with, who is business inclined.
Such a person must not be envious of your passion for enterprise and growth. But count yourself lucky if you have one or two, within your circle of friends - otherwise you will have to develop your mind, to decipher answers to nagging problems. And you must find answers.
In the case of honest partnership, it is much easier to arrive at quality

decisions. It is less lonely because the owners can rub minds and see things differently, to make more accurate decisions.
Partnership may not be your forte because of some inherent challenges, so you may have to be your own problem solver. However, bigger organizations make much better decisions but the board may suffer from what is called *GroupThink* as I had mentioned before.

Therefore, as a sole entrepreneur, you may not be doing badly, if you struggle with your decisions alone. Relevant forums on the Internet may give you some answers, to some nagging issues without you losing your anonymity, or you could join a professional club in town.

When you seek new staff, you need to discuss the *modus operandi* so that nothing surprises such prospects. Allow such interviewees ask questions during the recruitment process for clearer understanding.
On resumption, there will be indoctrination about the company's philosophy, goals, strategy and culture. He is expected to know most of what is documented in the manuals over time by heart. It makes it easy and clearer of what is expected.
Delegation must also be measurable of performance and there are many tools to get this done.

And again, as the business grows, the owner may need to hand over to a supervisor, who further manages the junior staff under him. If you choose to remain small, there is nothing wrong with it. It's all about your strategic vision. There are many small scale businesses, that just choose to maintain a particular level of activity and farm out some aspects of activities; yet they are very profitable.
For the typical business, there is always a desire to grow. From onset, the business is positioned to generate higher income, in line with the vision

of its founder.

So delegation allows the founder or the chief executive to coordinate all the units of the business in synergy with the organizational goals. When you delegate, you are able to see more broadly and to solve problems better. It also frees up time to brainstorm and to tweak ideas that will ensure everything works in harmony.

Watch Your Emotion

Let me share a personal experience where my being over sentimental that cost me a fortune, because I made an inappropriate decision about a business idea. This was a seed idea I had been nursing in my mind. Unknowingly, I simply killed it when it should have been birthed.

There was a time, years back; I suddenly realized I could turn an extra space in my office to start another branch of my photo studio business. I had sketched the plans for a while with the intention of employing a photographer, to man this unit while I carried on with my other endeavors. And I knew that would have been a good synergy to my primary business, since they would be within the same vicinity.

Now, all this while, there had been a vacant space at the ground floor of the same building as I was.

But in the same month I eventually had the resources to put up my studio, the vacant floor was taken by another business. I was happy that, whatever new business that was coming in could give us some traffic due to our proximity, since we shared the same premises.

But I was wrong. The new business happened to be a photo studio also. I was confused!

Anyway, if I may ask you;
what would you have done in my shoes, since my plan was at a completion stage?
Was it to abandon my long passion or go ahead and get mine opened to the public?

I didn't have a clear analysis for an answer.
I asked an acquaintance, a business owner what decision to make. He was not forthcoming as well.
So I felt since I didn't want my nursed idea of opportunity to be seen as a moral issue, I decided to kill that branch of my photo studio.
I looked elsewhere, at another part of the town to start the studio. The immediate synergy of having it under the same roof was lost.
Within my primary business office, rather than opening to the pedestrian public, I decided to change the marketing approach to servicing companies that needed industrial photography.
This area of photography basically is done at a client's location.
It pays quite well, but not as regular as it should be, when compared with portrait photography - with clients that could walk in more frequently.

But in retrospect, I realized a successful business man must be shrewd and stand by his ideas coming to full implementation, as long as it wasn't an illegal decision.
That is exactly, what I should have done.

I simply should have put up my own signage, stand firm on the ground and do my own thing. I did otherwise. And that was a stupid mistake.
The new guy was even unfriendly, when he realized the edge we had over our high caliber clients and the salient approach we used to get clients. If only he knew, the sacrifice I made on his behalf.
While the second studio was opened elsewhere for the public, another error of judgment I made, yet again, based on sentiments.

These two experiences happened in the same year, 2001. You must have read that earlier. We learn everyday as I have.
By the way, this year I noticed two new laundries - situated side by side- in my neighborhood. How will each survive?

Your Daily Grind

We must carry out daily activities when managing our enterprise, be it, a micro-enterprise or a conglomerate. The pattern or the routine is never standardized as most decisions and activities we undertake tend to be unique and organic.

We might have designed required schedules but there are occasions, the rules must be broken, that is being real. But all efforts must meet the set objectives.
We must be methodological, when we take these detours against the predefined schedules. Because without proper planning and schedule of operations, an organization would be run by our whims and caprices. That brings in indiscipline.
This would disrupt the collective system that ought to take the business far into the future.
We don't want to be haphazard in our daily operations. Of course there will always be exceptions, as I have said.

Now what does a business need on a regularly or on a daily basis? Some days, the routine work goes smoothly as envisaged. Other days, everything may seem to be disorganized, but you have to keep at it, to overcome. All the departments of your business must be attended to, at a designated period.

Chapter 16

Time In

Managing Customer Interface

This is the first interface between a business and prospective customers. The first line of interaction, where the business can win them over or not.

The customer-service interface comes in different shades, depending on the type of industry. You must ensure as a leader that you have put a proper structure in place. A daily monitoring must be put in the right perspective and your team must be clear about the implementation.

And if you are still working alone, you simply must do what increases your bottom line.

Here the company engages with the consumer, with the aim of a mutually rewarding experience. But it is a delicate unit in any business that goes beyond the obvious. As we tend to deal with fellow human beings, we will realize that our expectations of the public might be faulty. The imperative is that, we should be quick to hear them out, understand the customers very well, before we rush to conclusion. There are a lot of advantages on this manner of approach.

It is better to keep our own prejudice, hold on with our assumptions, before we engage with the customers.

Depending on the type of industry we operate in, we will get to know the character of our buying public in that industry. This is because consumers behave differently in different industries, when they want to make a purchase, irrespective of their economic power.

No wonder in many developing countries, in *sub-Saharan* Africa, it is shocking to telecoms companies that expensive mobile phones, are routinely bought by low income earners.

Some would rather starve and save, to go for these high-end smart phones.

Therefore, you must know your market and thereafter design an appropriate customer service platform that meets their expectation.

A client buying a piece of common furniture from you will behave in a particular way. He behaves differently when he sees professionals, such as a doctor or a lawyer. His interaction will be different with a bartender.

There are situations consumers could choose to be condescending, but well behaved elsewhere, depending on product or the positioning of the business outfit.

All these scenarios should be considered, when your front office or customer service team is interacting with a client; a must on your daily activities.

Your industry and how the market place perceives your enterprise or industry must be understood. This awareness, which to a large extent is psychological, should be ingrained into the minds of the staff, especially those coming from a different industry.

Business owners cannot afford but to understand the whimsical nature of their peculiar consumers. Of course, the different phases of the highs and lows of any enterprises, resonate with the market place and its perception of the business.

A prosperous and established business will tend to be more respected by consumers, than the one going through the teething period of infancy.

Therefore, a young business must manage its customer service very well, within its resources.

Juggling The Working Capital

Working capital is mostly the money and the stock of goods that the business needs for its routine activities. It varies widely across all types of businesses. It may be physical cash for some businesses and non-cash in nature. It may be needed on a daily basis, monthly, quarterly or as the case may be.

Whichever form it takes in your business, there is a need to estimate and keep such aside or have backup plans to make provisions when needed. No doubt, occasions might push you to take from your reserves. You might have cause to go for a short term credit by your supplier or raise an overdraft, to keep things smooth running.
However, discipline yourself to pay back, before it develops into a huge problem.

In essence it involves the cash flow management of your business. It also involves details about your stock movement. In the absence of adequate working capital, opportunities may be lost or losses are incurred.
Do note also that too much free money can kill your creativity.
That is one of the reasons, the first set of promoters of the dot.com failed. Exhaust your creativity and increase your sense of awareness before throwing money at every management challenge.

Being over stocked might also tie down the needed cash. There is a need to know the optimum amount of your supplies for a chosen period. Have you noticed newspaper vendors? How do they know the saleable number of copies to hold?

There is a theory called *The Newsboy Model*.
It is a variation of the *Economic Order Quantity* (EOQ) formula which is expected to reveal the right number of stocks that will serve the business within a time frame.
In arriving at this, you would have keyed in some numbers into the formula. I won't go into the details here. But now you know how to minimize wastages or over-stocking.

Talking about money, we should also realize that inadequate capital can stall most businesses, creating a situation of slow inertia. This can be frustrating to a business promoter who has identified opportunities she could tap into. She has to bid her time until she gets adequate funding. She would have to keep on tapping on the table or on the floor until that nagging dream becomes a reality, to serve.

Get Up From The Chair

On these last days of August 2016 as I write, *Facebook* Co-Founder, *Mark Zuckerberg* quietly slipped into my neigbourhood, just two streets away in *Yaba, Lagos*, Nigeria.
He came around to meet young indigenous developers. And he said he had learnt some things here. This was his reported first trip to the *sub-Saharan* Africa.
You are expected in business, to leave your comfort zone, to see where you can do things together with other enterprises. You cannot survive as an island. When companies leverage on each other's resources or assets, both can benefit including their customers.
Some owners are rather shy, with fear of being rebuffed to arrange an alliance. It should not be so.

The Big Secret: bring something of value to people, that is the only way they will hear you out.

If you lack the initiative due to your introversion or you do not have the energy, you can engage the services of a temporary assistant. He will venture out to where opportunities have been identified by you and you compensate accordingly.
One of the major reasons behind building a bridge across the business divide is to ultimately help your clients the more. You want them to buy more from you too. You can therefore introduce other services beyond your primary products or services you offer.

I had a friend who was into marketing digital satellite TV subscription. I knew he had a long list of customers and I tried to strike a deal with him for mutual benefits. He did not have to spend a kobo or a cent. He was to let me market my portraits photo business to his list of clients. But he wasn't enthusiastic about the extra money he would have made. He didn't have to lift a finger. I got instead only a trickle of referrals and he stopped. The idea died after that.
I felt he was not comfortable on my leveraging that idea. He would rather not take the free money or he didn't want to be helpful. I may be wrong. I looked elsewhere.

Why am I saying this? Maybe it is better to seek an amiable stranger to seek an alliance for mutual benefits.
Develop alliances with other much endowed businesses which serve your niche. That will quickly increase your sales, giving you an edge over your competition.
But it is a lot of work that demands a good interpersonal skill.

However, be aware that many business owners are protective of their customers from being introduced to just any external business proposal. It is better to go after businesses that are on the same level as yours, so that you don't waste your time. Yet you must also spare some time for bigger businesses, as the leverage would be much higher. Create a potpourri of target companies. It is fun.

For those that hesitate, let them try the idea for free and go back for a feedback, if they had any gains. Alliances are very widespread in business. You see airlines doing it with hotels to ensure their customers are provided diverse beautiful things of interest.

So as an entrepreneur, you can use this concept at your local level. A budding software developer might approach a popular restaurant that serves his niche market. An App that could benefit the patrons and their two businesses, in a tripartite.

This is an example of an underground marketing – guerrilla marketing, some would call it.

Lastly, before you approach any business, consider what they would see as tangible benefits from this relationship. You plan on this before you approach them.

Getting Your Work Done

The only expendable item that is given to the rich and the poor, in equal measure, is our 24 hours we have in a day. How an entrepreneur uses these hours is very important.

By simply planning for the next day; just write on a piece of paper what you would do from the previous day. It is a useful habit to develop, but it gets broken on few occasions. Not to worry.

The last thing in the evening before you retire; write down - from the most difficult item.

Follow the list in a sequence. Start from the most important and urgent item and work the list. It is a powerful way of getting things done on a daily or weekly basis. The technique allows you achieve your objectives quickly. It encourages the best use of time and it forces personal discipline.

You will eventually realize it makes you feel better, as you tick each milestone covered, on your list. Never mind your falling back at times, since you are not a robot. There are days we ignore the list and simply allow the soul to take the initiative. There are times, too, we don't finish up the daily schedule; we simply roll over to the next day.

But you know the adherence to the list makes for more efficiency. So, strive we should, to optimize our time and energy, as entrepreneurs or business leaders.

The Modern Day Time-Stealers

Technology may steal our precious time – as a self-imposed deprivation. It doesn't come in a stealth manner but we fall for its hypnotic appeal. We become heavily dependent. But we have the power to manage it.

From the minute by minute of checking emails, to wanting to read - whether others have given us - a *"like"* on our *Facebook* postings. The immediacy of gadgets at our finger tips has seriously killed some aspect of our humanity.

Arguably worse than the advent of television. Time management for fruitful engagements has become a struggle. Anyway, smart business owners know better. They embrace technology but they prioritize their time with their usage. But we can overcome by being conscious of all this and managing them effectively. I fell for it. But I soon had recoil for good. I am better off.

For instance, for my weekly exercise of long walks, there are no endowed

gadgets on my body. I don't rush to pick a call, even while I may nurse a call from *Oprah Winfrey, Bill Gates, Warren Buffet* or *Mo Ibrahim*…
In other words make the best use of your time. Don't kill your brain by dwelling too much on these devices. Engage other human beings by physically being in their presence. Touch them and discuss about life and your endeavors.

Today, we must be disciplined about the use of the ubiquitous - and sometime distracting - gadgets found around us. The Internet, the radio, the TV, the phones, just name them…
While we need them, we must define the most sensible way of usage, at the work place even at home. We must discipline ourselves from their seductive nature. I advise we use them with wisdom but we must not allow technology to steal our 24 hours! Technology is a two edged sword.

Talking about friends and other time-wasters; do not allow them disturb you at work. The place of work can't be an appropriate place to fraternize and this applies to the staff too. I presume in some climes, this is a well known aspect of their culture. Time for work and time for play are distinct and therefore should be respected by any serious business owner.

Chapter 17

Time Out

The Little Exercise
There are times when one chooses to reflect on the business and stretch the body, literally speaking.
I do reserve a time, to shut my eyes and just let my mind wander, while at my seat. At times, I would get up and simply pace around in my office or leave the premises and walk across the street for about ten minutes and come back. This habit is not a daily occurrence though, but just to remove some cobwebs from the brain, to think straight. An entrepreneur is a different animal, each one with a unique ritual all in a bid to attain excellence.

When you can squeeze the time, a little physical exercise might just be. Bending down slowly to touch your toes. I also do my slow-but-deep conscious breathing exercise. Because when we are engrossed in the task in front of us, we tend to breathe less or we don't do it properly.

Our physical posture - the body - is also conformed to one position throughout the day. This could give us some bodily pains. It could also result in a permanent disability in the future. Some may develop piles or hemorrhoids because of their too heavy sedentary life style.
I stretch my limbs slowly. I remove my shoes and use my hands to gently curve my feet. I lift my facial skin and massage the muscles gently.

Make gentle twists and turn of my neck and other joints. Five minutes, I am done. Then I am ready to go back to the task at hand.
I eat light lunch rather than heavy because if I do otherwise, I may feel sleepy. Post-noon is the best period of my creativity—when I am at my peak. It was not like that many years back. *I don't know.* The body has changed. Yours will certainly be different. So know what works for you.

Napping For Productivity

An entrepreneur must ensure he maintains an alert state of mind.
There are occasions when you are deprived of sleep, and you will know it. Find the next opportunity to take a break and have a real catnap!
You might feel it is smart to struggle through the tasks at hand, but that wouldn't yield your productive best at your groggy state.
The time used to tune up your body system is never a waste of time. The human body being a system needs its own timely and proper input, to give peak human performance.

If you are an elderly entrepreneur, be realistic about the limiting circumstances around you. You can only do much as an organic entity. As you get older, this organic resource - your being - reduces in power. In that wise, it behoves on you to plan your time more carefully and re-strategize as I have mentioned earlier.

Our make-up differs; therefore planning your time, to meet personal and business objectives can't be like others. You will always know how your body feels. Health-wise, our body *"speaks"* to us in unique ways. If we *"listen"*, we will know what it is saying to avoid a burnout.

Some of us can do with just a few hours of sleep, while others may need extra hour of mental rest for peak performance. Even in your nuclear

family, every member has different sleeping patterns. Though as one gets older, you tend to sleep less.
The occasional few minutes of catnap, if allowed, in the office environment, has been proved to recharge the body, to work for many more hours.

Lest I forget, when it comes to feeding, we need to watch what and how we eat. Watch your meals, especially the heavy breakfast that could make some people feel sleepy during the morning hours, as you start your day at work.
For me, there are occasions I have a short nap when I arrive in the office, in the morning. I don't feel ashamed to say this, because it works for me. I have discovered that even if I had had many hours of sleep overnight, once I arrive in the office, I can't be at my mental peak immediately. Maybe it's because of driving through the rush hour traffic.
Fifteen to thirty minutes will do the trick. If the time is not broken, on waking up, I could work for many unbroken hours into the rest of the day.
It works for me, but maybe not for you!
So don't struggle with that drowsiness. Just get that short nap.

Feeling The Blues

The body may be wiling but the soul may feel otherwise. How do we resolve this reality at the workplace?
I will say here that, there are some days you just don't feel like doing anything. You just don't want to do any work.
This can apply to anybody, from the factory floor technician to the CEO. Adjustments must be made to recoup the lost days, though. We are not all robots, even machines break down.

However there must be devices - either tangible or intangible - that must be laid out to prevent or reduce this human weakness. This is to forestall whatever human error that could arise when we choose to force ourselves to do the work.
Imagine an airline pilot, lab technologist or a chef whose mind wanders away from the task at hand.

From my personal experience, when I am caught in this mood, despite what I have on my list, I have discovered it is better, one takes a break. You might feel guilty, but struggle with that state of mind as you may, the results of your forced efforts would not yield the best of results. You get refreshed but come back to your tasks.
This pause could be a few minutes, an hour or even a day. It all depends on how you are feeling the blues.

Where feasible allow your staffs who are equally stressed, to be refreshed too. But watch out for ungrateful and opportunistic employees who just choose to be lazy.

Chapter 18

Dealing With Problems

Steps To Problem Solving

On a daily basis in our personal lives and in business, problems are expected to be recognized and solved. This is a reality of our existence. We solve problems daily.

But getting the best solutions can be very intimidating at times. Since we can't fold our arms, we must discover a pattern of resolving our nagging issues. Many popular methods are abounding, on how to carry out the necessary exercise of finding optimized solutions.

The first thing to be done is to write down what the obvious problems are. The trick is to discover the root cause which might not be obvious, until we dig deeper.

As you write them down, be aware of your emotional state which might becloud your accurate judgment.

An over-excited state of mind may prevent an objective outcome. Therefore, you have to calm your mind and following scientific method. The exercise has been successful for me, for over 25 years, since I discovered the technique, way back in the *MBA School*.

It can also be applied to your personal life. Though I believe not all concepts are perfect for all situations, there will always be exceptions in our world. Nature demonstrates that daily. That is he only *caveat* I would give.

Having said that, you might go contrary to this methodology. Your well tuned hunches or gut feeling could give you a more fruitful resolution. Your prior experience in decision making could be an asset.
You know yourself better.

It is a methodological and a logical flow, which goes like this:

Determine what you suspect is the root or the central issue. For instance if you are agitated about low patronage in your business, you need to find out the root cause and not the discouraging figure of a loss in your books.

After this, you must determine what are the relevant factors that could be associated with this major problem. They could be many. You list them. It could be bad customer service, which keeps them away. It could be the entrance of a new competitor with better offerings serving your niche market. It could also be the general economic factor or recession in your country. *Be true to yourself, no matter how unpalatable.*

The next phase is to list all the alternative courses of actions, that is, the solutions that could be taken. However at this stage, you must identify the advantages and disadvantages of each penciled down solution or course of actions, so identified.
If it is a problem about staffing, you may be considering whether to hire or fire. You may decide hiring an unskilled employee or you go for a skilled manpower.
You will consider the remuneration involved, in either situation with reference to the financial strength of the business and expected income by virtue of this decision. It could be a decision on whether the company should relocate to another city or leave the premises.

Then the next step is to discuss all these alternatives with important members of your team.
If you are alone, you will do it yourself to think through these alternatives. Or you may table them before a trusty mentor or friend, who must be business minded.
At this juncture, you will know the alternatives to jettison based on your set guidelines.
Eventually, you will reach a few set of conclusions.
It is now you can pick the best solution, subject to your earlier set parameters. Finally you must act decisively and immediately on the best solution chosen. Keep plan B or C, should plan A fails, eventually.

Problem analysis is subject to the sensitivity and the urgency of the problem at hand. Therefore, accurate attention must be given to address these issues. This is part of the daily grind of any going-concern.

To the naïve – on the outside, a business might look as if no feathers are rustled, but that could be contrary to the reality. As we say in the *Yoruba* culture in Nigeria, *"the chicken actually perspires but for the feathers that wouldn't allow us see the sweat-beads"*
The executives or the owners of such businesses know when to quickly douse the fire, before it becomes an inferno. That is what they are paid to do, anyway. To solve problems!

The chap on the factory floor may erroneously envy or wonder why executives are paid so much. *agree many are over-compensated.*
He won't know that executives are expected to be cracking hard nuts and do more in enterprise building.
With experience an organization knows how to solve its problems, based on its past failures and successes. It gets better with time.

Recognizing The Red Flag

How do you know when the red flag is hoisted, that is, when the business demands urgent attention?

Are sales becoming infrequent despite all efforts? You will need a mental pause. Do not panic. Simply revert to the problem identification process for the best solution. If you have a smart team, then it becomes easier to resolve. Otherwise you may need a fresh eye from outside the company. A seasoned business oriented friend or mentor, if you have one.

It is very possible that no matter how much you analyze on your own, the culprit or the root cause of the problems might escape your mind's eye. We all have blind spots when it comes to some judgments. It may be obvious but hidden to you.

This is where at times, an external business consultant may help out - who has actually run a business. *So let me hear from you if you will need my help, ok?*

Could the problem be an important external factor, outside the control of your company?
How do you know when the red flags are up?
You will simply know when your short and medium term objectives are not being met. And you must act, to rectify things in a decisive manner.

There are different scenarios I could conjure up here. Examples are many and varied.
Could be that the sales are dwindling? Your major suppliers of raw materials are about leaving town? Maybe a sudden increase in price, is affecting your production cost? Maybe the quality of your product or

service can no longer catch up with the new trend?
It may also be due to inadequacy of the working capital, resulting in lost opportunities, while staffs are being owed salaries.

Be aware that some problems may come up that are beyond our comprehension and our efforts to rectify them may fall us. We will need courage and deep introspection to know the right steps to take. It is not the time to panic.

I leave you with this. Watch your worrying plate closely but keep an eye on the business goals. Do not let the boat capsize. Be decisive, whatever it takes legally. Do something. Don't be sorry later. Be happy.

Want Timely Information About My New Books and Free Resources?

- Visit and signup for my newsletter at **www.muyiwaosifuye.com** for **helpful** articles, downloadable audios, podcasts, videos and more.

- For your next **Management Consulting and Business Advisory Services**: send an email to mosifuye@gmail.com and copy contact@muyiwaosifuye.om

- **My Business Tips And Insights**
  www.twitter.com/rbizchat

- **My Watering Hole: Join Me With Others**
  www.facebook.com/StomRuby

About The Author

'MUYIWA OSIFUYE was born in Lagos, in January 1960.
He is the CEO of Stom and Ruby Services – a boutique Management Consulting and Business Advisory services amongst other businesses.

He has a degree in Optometry (1984) from the University of Benin, Nigeria.
He has an MBA – specialising in Marketing & Finance (1991) from the University of Lagos, Nigeria and also a Diploma (2002) in Professional Photography from the New York Institute of Photography, USA.
He lives in Lagos, Nigeria.

www.ingramcontent.com/pod-product-compliance
Lightning Source LLC
Chambersburg PA
CBHW070241190526
45169CB00001B/259